2018
Found Poems and Weather Reports

2018
Found Poems and Weather Reports

Lyman Grant

ALAMO BAY PRESS
SEADRIFT•AUSTIN

Copyright © 2020 by Lyman Grant

All rights reserved. No part of this book may be reproduced in any form without permission in writing from the publisher, except by a reviewer who may quote brief passages in a review.

Cover: Eugène Isabey, *A Storm Off the Normandy Coast*.
Book Design: ABP

For orders and information:
Alamo Bay Press
Pamela Booton, Director
825 W 11th Ste 114
Austin, Texas 78701
pam@alamobaypress.com
www.alamobaypress.com

Library of Congress Control Number: 2020932844
ISBN: 978-1-943306-18-3

*For those who
will clean up
the mess,
with apologies.*

"Is this," they say, "the nonsense
        That we expect of poets?"
"Where is the Picturesque?"
        "Where is the vertigo of emotion?"
"No! his first work was the best."
        "Poor Dear! He has lost his illusions."
                —Ezra Pound, "Salutations the Second," from *Lustra*

Let the birds do the singing.
        —Nicanor Parra

Spring comes, summer;
cool clear weather; heat, rain. . . .
        —Jane Kenyon "Now Where?"

a weathered monument to some of the dead.
        —Natasha Trethewey, "Elegy for the Native Guards"

And we could talk about what happened to God.
        —Robert Bly, "Plan for a Year"

Puppet. I'm not a puppet. You're the puppet.
        —Donald J. Trump

Contents

1	Prologue
5	January
23	February
33	March
49	April
65	May
81	June
99	July
115	August
127	September
143	October
157	November
169	December
189	Epilogue
193	Notes
209	Acknowledgments
211	About Lyman Grant

2018
Found Poems and Weather Reports

Prologue
Lines from December 2017

you complain about process
                    when you are
                                        losing
every single one of us
                    assumed

                                                    we were listening to a crass
standup act
                    well
                                if it must be onward
to the end
                        let's get
            there in a hurry:

                                            I need shooters
                            the kingdom of heaven
            is at hand
                    because
                                if not at hand

                                                                it
                    is nowhere
        we drove
                through
    a wall of flames
                                we'll have borders on top of borders
                    and
        what might be going on
                        today
                                in our country
                        in which people are stoking
a sort of victim
                complex
                                                among white men
                    holy infant
            so tender   and mild
                                                        it's
seen
as what happens   when you're

2018   3

                        just
                            being   one
                      of the guys
                   with more
         than 20 million
people
             submitting

January

1.1
Too old
For it
Anymore
Bed before fireworks
And the descending ball
Cold/a cold
Eight degrees/Nyquil

Home: Harrisonburg, VA
Monday on the road
Portent
For what
How long
Packing the back
Of the Kia Soul
Turned at the honking
Of a V
Of a dozen geese
Happiness almost
They're cold
Also

Theraflu mileage south
Shenandoah Valley
Calvary attacks/swords
And inward angry voices
Cold Fuck this cold
Flank and reform
Just drive
Schizo mix on Iphone
Daft Punk w/Paul Williams
   A painter in my mind
   Tell me what you see
   A tourist in a dream
   Where do I belong?
Van Morrison/Christine
   McVey
Carpenters
   What I've got some people

Call the blues

Bristol
Knoxville
Crossville

Nashville/the motherland
Driving into a ring of fire
Billboards for Patsy Cline
And Johnny Cash
Comfort Inn/Memory Foam
Hum the song
   And we'll take
   A cup of kindness
   Yet

1.2
The morning begins
   North Korean Leader
   Kim Jong Un
   Just stated
   That the 'Nuclear Button
   Is on his desk
   At all times'
   Will someone
   From his depleted
   And food starved regime
   Please inform him
   That I too
   Have a Nuclear Button
   But it is a much bigger
   & more powerful
   One than his
   And my Button works!
   @realdonaldtrump

Still
Cold/3 degrees
After motel breakfast
Sausage patty/biscuit/gravy

In a plastic bowl with a plastic
    fork
Colleen and I visit
National Cemetery
Long beautiful rows stand
In order at attention
For what for eternity/for
    respect
I tell my mother and father
That their grandson
William is getting married
In five days
Seems like somebody
Ought to tell them
Lt. Col. Grant salutes
Birdie smiles sadly
I think she still regrets
Dying in her forties
She could have seen
William grow up

Back on 40 West
Straight lines double lanes
To Memphis
Set the cruise control and
    watch
Manifest Destiny roll by/
All the way to Sun Records
And Graceland
And the Lorraine Motel
Don't stop
Got to keep moving
Point out to Theo
A couple dozen geese
In and out of formation
Everybody's cold/heading
    south

Colleen and I switch off
Every hundred or so miles
Then to Little Rock/30 South
Then to Texarkana
Dark and still cold
Colleen cultures herself with
    NPR
I am taking a temp vacation
From Trump
Ears plugged
I am looking at the bare trees
Listening to "Bare Trees"
    I was alone in the cold
    On a winter's day
But I am not alone
Gratitude

1.3
The eggs at the Comfort Inn
In Texarkana Texas
Are fake mealy
And the coffee watered down
Still below freezing

Once we hit the road
The day seems better
Cruise Control at 75 mph
We make good time
To Colleen's Dad's
Place in the country
For short visit and
To take him to lunch
We discover the cold
Has broken a water pipe
Outside the house
A series of puddles emerging
From under the leaves
In the grove of oaks
Behind the house
Like Rorschach archipelagos
At 85 and post three strokes
His problem-solving skills

Are slow and muddied
The plumber an old friend
Of his has done a lot
Of work on the place
After an hour or so
And unanswered calls
We find him out in his fields
He agrees to drive out
To evaluate/confirm
We have a leak that needs
To be repaired
Glad I am not digging
Into wet cold muck
This afternoon

In Austin
Hours later
Jacob and William and I
Head down to The Chili Parlor
For beer and dinner
One of my old hangouts
That I am missing
Just wanted to visit
One more time/might never
Get to again/who knows
All the old places
In Austin
Are shutting down
Closing
Can't compete
Pay the rising rents
In the bathroom
I remember the graffiti
I learned there in the 70s:
    To be is to do: Socrates
    To do is to be: Sartre
    Do be do be do: Sinatra
For years I introduced
Linking and active verbs
With that bit of wisdom

Now nobody gets the joke

1.4
Many miles south
The cold wave's ebbing
Wake up to blue skies
And high 30's
Going to be in the 50's today

So I am four days into this
And it is hitting me
How much I have
To leave out
We think our days
Are boring and tedious
In need of action
And emotion
But a lot happens
When nothing happens

We traveled 1200 miles
In three days without really
Pushing it
That's a lot
Of trees and grass
And asphalt
Starbucks and Cracker Barrels
Exxons and Shells
Noticed briefly
Many of them
Into our vision and out
Noted discarded
Tang of lemon drop
Burn of a Fireball
Something for the mouth
To do
While nothing/everything
Passes by
Somebody farts

We say nothing
But roll down window
For a few seconds
Just moving
Through our day

What am I going to do
With this
What is this
A book a project a folly
Once I start doing it

I have never been
A diligent journal keeper
I have started
And abandoned
More than I remember
I think I get bored
With myself when I write
Only to myself
I find myself more interesting
When I am writing to
… "you"
Who the hell are "you"

One thing
I did not write about
That happened
Each of the three
Preceding days
Is that
At different times
In the day
I thought
To open the laptop
And type out something
I don't say anything about that
Because writing about the day
Is supposed to be separate
From the day isn't it

Isn't that the danger
That I will write
About writing (like now)
Or even write about writing
About writing
(like now) and it is endless

I wrote the following a week
    or so
Ago when thinking about
    what
2018 would be about
May as well drop it in here
    Put my hands to work on
    keyboard
    play scales
    each note's value pressed
    Honor Truth Piety Justice,
    Courage Love Discipline
        Faith
yes yes I know
These dull abstractions thud
    flat
"In this modern world of
    today"
(student notebook
    assignment
due in one year)

Amuse me
"How do I get to Carnegie
    Hall"

I don't know
What any of that means
Really
But I have a goal
To live a life
That is Good
In that very old-fashioned

Lyman Grant

And traditional way
And that what I write
Should be Good
You know capital letter
Good
Because
It flows
From a clean source
You know
Clean beautiful healthful
Water
From a stream
In the mountains
Where the air is pure

Is there such a place

I just typed all this sitting
Cross-legged on the floor
At a friend's house
Where we are staying
I have to
Get up
And move around

1.5
Warming up
Day before big day
Just errands
A haircut and beard trim
Picking up a small keg
Of Karbach Kolsh
Helping out at my ex-
Wife's house where
The rehearsal dinner will occur
Tonight
Icing down the beer
The white wine champagne
And sodas

Taking Colleen to her favorite
Quick food restaurant
P-Terry burger for Theo
His favorite
He has missed this burger
Terribly
Picking up pies
Made by a friend
From our old church
Pie
What says home
And love
Better than pie
There's a scene in *Matlock*
(Am I really going to name
Matlock in a serious poem)
About his enjoying pie
There's a story
About my first father-in-law
About his eating eight slices
Of pie at his in-laws in the
    forties
In Canada farm land
Pie I love pie all kinds of pie
Dressing driving back
To my ex's

People people people
Happy faces smiles
Handshakes
The back really hurt tonight
Had to find chairs to sit in
All through the night
William and Kati have many
Wonderful friends
That means
They are wonderful
But I knew that

My duty

Begin the toasts
Patriarch and all that
Finished remarks with this bit
Of language:
    Love can be a vital
    Demanding and delicate
    Emotion
    And it seems to me
    That you two
    Have protected its delicacy
    Respected its demands
    And cherished its vitality
    I have great respect
    For how you have nurtured
    Your love for each other
    I wish you a marriage
    That is as romantic
    And as conscientious
    As your courtship

Then I could relax
Went back to where
We are staying and
Took some left over
Pain pills and lay on the floor
Until it didn't hurt anymore

1.6
Trump begins the day
Tweeting unendingly
    "(1) Now that <u>Russian collusion</u>
    After one year
    Of intense study
    Has proven
    To be a total hoax
    On the American public
    The Democrats and their
        lapdogs
    The Fake News Mainstream
        Media
    Are taking out
    The old Ronald Reagan
        playbook
    And screaming mental
        stability
    And intelligence…..
    (2) ….Actually,
    Throughout my life,
    My two greatest assets
    Have been <u>mental stability</u>
    And being
    Like really smart
    Crooked Hillary Clinton
    Also played these cards
    Very hard and
    As everyone knows
    Went down in flames
    I went from VERY
        successful
    Businessman
    To top T.V. Star…..
    (3) ….to President
    Of the United States
    (on my first try)
    I think that would qualify
    As not smart
    But genius….
    And a <u>very stable genius</u>
    At that!"
    @realdonaldtrump

I should say something
About the wedding
But I could write a novel
About this day
If I really dug in
Weddings are the meeting
    places

Of past present and future
Regrets and joys and fantasies
The first wife the ex-wife
Of thirteen years
And the son we have together
All he represents
That joy those mistakes
That grief this relief
It isn't his to carry
All those stories
That are usually effaced
Because he's been split
When he and I
Are together
The memories between us
Are only ours
When she and he
Are together
The memories between them
Are only theirs
He is always a half
Or maybe he is doubled
Twice the fund
Of memories
I live most days of my years
With her excised
My life bracketed
A tree with burned cavities
And scarred at the hole
Left by lightning fire
But I have also erased
A portion of my son's life
From him when he is
With me
And so also I guess
With her
And this has taken so long
To say and
It is only one beam of light
In a day glaring brightly

One son a new husband
One son a best man
One son a groomsman
And in perfect blue suits
My sisters their husbands
A niece husband two
    daughters
A nephew and wife
A family when we hear
So much about broken families
I wear the Grant tartan
Tie and scarf
"Stand Fast!"

I barely remember my father
At my own wedding

Hell of a thing to think
That the greatest thing
One has done
Is survive this long
And the hardest thing
One can do now
Is survive a bit longer
For my other sons

1.7-1.9
Colleen and Theo to airport
So they can start
Their school years again
Next drive back to
Birmingham
With Jacob in rain
He is returning to college
A couple weeks early
Cause he can stay with a friend
And do some day labor
For spending cash
Sounds dumb to say this

But Jacob is a good driver
It's cold raining hard
Most of the way
We drive through the day
Into the night and morning
He drives the late shift
And I trust him
At the frat house
I sleep on a mattress
On the floor and leave
Early decide to go slow
And take two days back
Home still raining
Motel room
Alabama-Georgia
NCAA Championship game
Don't know why I watch
I watch so little sports
But tonight is why we watch
A young man emerges
From the ranks of the team
And becomes a hero
The next day
The final 200 miles
I linger on the old highway
And see the little Virginia
Towns that the interstate
Ignores

1.10
I will let today go by
Without any reports
(oops I guess this is a report)
But I have to give you the
    reader
A little breather I think
There is no way
That I can write fully
About everyday

Even "I" who is living this
Is not interested enough
To read about everything
That I make happen
Or that happens to me
That is all
For today

1.11
Today
New job day
Always seems that no matter
How much money I make
I don't make enough
Colleen and I are such children
With money
I am ashamed of that
I did one thing right
At least I think
Set myself up for state
Retirement 40 years ago
Just kept putting money in
Stayed at the same job
With same school
Played it safe
No monkey business
Get rich quick schemes
But I did three things
That screwed me
    1. Divorce:
Divorce always costs
And all the money put
Into that marriage and
Houses gone
    2. Remarried
A younger woman
Without a profession
Without much prospect
Then of helping support

The family financially
    3. Began having
More children in my forties
So now in my sixties
I still need to pay for college
Colleen in college
Jacob in college
And Theo in high school
And then more college
    4. Should add
These are just facts
Regardless
I would commit
All three "mistakes"
Again

All this to say today I began
A second part-time job
Eastern Mennonite University
Hourly not so much money
Not even a couple thou
More a month
(First part-time job
Is on-line teaching
With my old school
(Starts in a couple weeks))
Don't know what new job
Will entail
So weird beginning again
In a new place not knowing
Anyone
The irony is that I used to say
My dream in retirement
Would be to be
That old man professor
Who sits in the student lounge
(Not creepy really)
And talks with students
About whatnot
Friendly supportive

Encouraging
That fantasy that professor
Who doesn't have anything left
To lose
And so teaches as a professor
Ought to teach
To the students' souls
Not to their resumes
The irony now
Can I do that
Did I really mean that
Is that really me or a symptom
Of my broken psyche
A need
Not a gift

I hear I will tutor a number
International students
Today Trump says,
    Why do we want
    all these people
    from 'shithole countries'
    coming here?

1.12
Fri.
Finally I am admitting
That I will be living in Virginia
For the foreseeable future
Drive to the DMV
To get my VA driver's license
WTF the DMV is closed
For Lee-Jackson Day
VA's FU to MLK day
Which is next Mon.
Incredible

1.15
Haven't wanted to begin

Again too much stuff
To say to keep up
Too little happening
That's inspiring
Time goes by so slowly
Still waking up feeling
Lousy take some pills
Shoot saline solution
Into my nostrils
Swig some DayQuil
Dress in slacks and button
   down
And wait to drive off
At 11:40
To be at my new job
At 12:00
Rough life
Nothing much going on
At work getting settled
Writing emails to announce
Who I am and that I am *here*
Make some appointments
For some class visits so
Grad students can check me
   out
Decide if I am a helpful type
Can they use me
To make the grade
Am I so cynical just tired
In my almost old age
Of worrying about who/what
Others read upon me
It's not even
What I project anymore
It's not Aristotle or Cicero
And ethos and character
And all that
Am I likeable
Is the only question
To be likeable

Or not to be
Likeable at all
All I want to do is show
Them how cool our language
Really is and all the fun stuff
We can do with it
So that's four hours
Of trying to be
The professional
That I think
Others think
I should be
Why not just be myself
Because
I think I have become
Someone who figured out
What life is for him
(And what does hope and
   aspiration
Have to do with an old man)
And I don't know
Do I suffer
Fools easily
Do I think a lot
Of people are fools
Smile can I help?

Home and the cabbage soup
I made yesterday MLK Day
So Colleen and Theo
Have no school and
Theo got to spend
The afternoon skiing
Watching the news
Two hours

Then Colleen and I drive to
   Bridgewater
To hear "Pulitzer Prize
Winning Columnist

Lyman Grant

At the *Washington Post*
Eugene Robinson"
That's how he's always
    introduced
He's always introduced that
    way
Nice talk but shallow
I think Robinson
Is a feeler not a thinker
He emotes his way
Toward the Truth
(Which he said
He does not think
Exists objectively
But I think he actually does
    think
It is there for us to find
Or at least get close to)
So he tells some stories
That don't lead to much
Other than us trusting
His experience
He doesn't have a truth
He is selling
He has an experience
He is letting us
Feel with him
Here in front of several
Hundred mostly white liberals
He keeps a lot to himself
I don't think
He trusts us
Some Black kids ask questions
About race racism
And I think Robinson
Sounds more like a parent
Keep working
Don't despair
Name it if you see it
Study history

Good advice but not
Dangerous advice
Not I-don't-have-anything-to-
    lose advice
Middle-class advice

Two and a half hours
There and back
An almond butter sandwich
And decaf
Random surfing on the
    television
Rachel Maddow and X-Files
And CNN

10:00 time for bed but here
I am typing this   well
At least I got out of bed and
Started on this ridiculous
    project
Again

1.20
"Trump's Shutdown"
Seems to me that we
Ought to be calling
This fiasco
"McConnell's Shutdown"
The Republicans keep wishing
To exclude all others
From contributing
To the governance
Of these here United States
Which, of course,
Are not united

Other than that
Beautiful day
60 degrees and sunny

Trip with Colleen
To the Saturday farmer's
　market
For eggs and leeks
And to the popcorn store
For National Popcorn Day
Two for one bags
Of flavored popcorn
Reading a novel on CIA
And cyber espionage
And thinking about a poem
About a Bruegel painting
That maybe I will write

1.23
I suppose it is good
That our lives
Are not like lizard's tails
And when some god
Has yanked at us too hard
And ripped off
A few years
Maybe if we are patient
Slowly
Those years come back to us
Green and hopeful
Maybe different from before
But maybe not
Who knows
Because
We would begin to think
When will this end
Does this adventure
Ever wrap
Well it does
Eventually
Nicanor Parra
Has finally died
That's proof

1.25
WASHINGTON —
President Trump ordered
the firing
last June of Robert S.
　Mueller III
the special counsel
overseeing the Russia
　investigation
according to four people
told of the matter
but ultimately backed down
after the White House
counsel threatened to resign
rather than carry out the
　directive.
The New York Times

1.27
Where have I been
All week/days passed
In winter's drudge
Doing my little job
Of tutoring grad students
Which while I'm at it
Is perfectly agreeable
Monitoring students
In my distance learning
Creative writing
And humanities classes
I guess
I should remember
That I had a low-grade illness
For a couple of weeks
Inducing day-time naps

Yesterday
Finally got my car
Registered in Virginia

Three weeks
Four trips to DMV
Four times standing
In lines Geez

Did a Bruegel poem
Submitted
And that led somehow
To writing five poems
About/around/reacting to
Russell Lee photographs
And those submitted
While I was at it
And three of my December
Poems about arias
Why not?

I am submitting poems
Because I am lonely
Because I want someone
To know that I am still
Alive and kicking
All my friends
Are in Texas/
    All my exes
    live in Texas
Don't have the dough
To travel
To a couple of spring
Writer's gatherings I like

Dropping a rock into a well

I miss my writing friends
Who writes in this town
Splash

Last night William wrote me
    I got to argue today
    that a big problem

we have with our health
science IRB is that we don't
have enough people
who've been trained
in the humanities.
It was taken pretty seriously
by our co-chair.
Thanks Dad!

How do we keep
An open mind
About having
Open minds

So many reasons
These days
Parents can find
To tell their children
To forget the arts
Forget culture
Opt for safety
And security
Thinking at least
The kind of thinking
That arts and history
And literature teaches
Does not reward quickly
Why can't humans be
Engineers accountants
And live
With contradictions

Going to see *The Post*
This afternoon with Colleen

1.29
Dear Sir
I saw your letter
To the editor

You seem very upset
Over the fact that some
People at the university
Here are indicating
Which pronouns
They prefer others
Use when addressing
Them bull shit
More or less
You say
Because one is born
With a gender
And no mind games
Can change that
I wanted to write
A response to you
And have it published
In the newspaper
But
I don't do things
Like that
And I don't want
You and other idiots
To be thinking
About some retaliation
You can direct
Toward me

But you end your rant
With a statement
That asserted that
Mind cannot override
Reality/That the Mind
Must conform to Reality
Not the other way around
I guess you are saying
The Mind cannot
Erase a Penis or a Gina

My letter

Would have said
Sir or Madame
You are an idiot
Living in the wrong
Century/First
You forget that one
Person's reality
≠ the Big Reality
And therefore mind
With the little m
Those processes
In your head ≠ Reality
And Mind
(whatever that is)
≠ reality
Sorry it doesn't
Or we would not have
Crime witnesses
Saying they saw
Different people or
Different events
Or different political
Parties or even
Be having this conversation

Second you forget "Language"
And we know
That language is unstable
Language ≠ Reality
Or reality
Or we would not have
Different languages
Or figures of speech
Or idioms that make
People with different
Languages or dialects
See the world differently
You may be a fundamentalist
At heart/and you may
Then say

Jesus is the Light/Well
There we have it
Don't we
Where is that light switch
You unliteral dipstick
And the really big issue
Is that your mind ≠ Mind
Because the main way
That mind can approach
Mind is through Language
And oops Language
Is unstable.

O yes I forgot
Third your glorious mind
Exists in a body
And therefore
Is subject to all sorts
Of sensations and
Biochemical processes
Some of which we are
Able to attach
Some kind of language to
And some of which
We can merely feel
And be in awe of
(As in speechless)
Or be confused by
That really screws around
With what reality the mind
Is able to see and understand.
And anyway Mr. Philosopher
Which is stronger the mind
Or the cock or the pussy
What if her mind says "girl"
And her cock says
You're right"

Finally
Why do you

Fucking care
What pronoun a person
Wishes to be called by
Why do you someone
Obviously enthralled
By his or her
Own sense of agency
Wish to deny
Another person his or her
Or their own agency?
Are you not
Even man enough
To let people be
Themselves?

2018

February

2.4
Cold morning
Somewhere under freeze point
Colleen stayed home
While I walked
A couple of blocks
To Emanuel Episcopal
For Rite 1
Which means no music
Have to say
Things were a little droney
What was it
People didn't get enough sleep
Or is it that
There are just so many grey
Hairs in the congregation
But things picked
Up with the second oldest
Metaphor in the world
The first is darkness
The second is light

Candlemas/mass
40 days since the birth
Of Christ
Time for his presentation
And Leviticus says
For the mother's purification
Well so much for that stuff
Today's celebration falls
To Simeon and
   a light for revelation
   to the Gentiles
   and for glory
   to your people Israel.
And the question is
Will I be a light
Will I let the light
That is in me
Shine

The body and blood
Consumed
I pick up the gift
Of a candle
From the rector
And leave

I walk outside
Into a light snowfall
Lawns are white
Tiny icy flakes
Tap and tickle
My cheeks
There's no word
Really for how it feels
Not a prick or a tingle
Not a strike or a pat

As I make my way home
The silence sings
In time with my steps
I stop I start I pause
Letting the moment
Be
A moment
It has been snowing
The entire service
I guess
It is snowing now
And I am alone
In it

2.6
Cold morning
Mid-20's
Who is this kid
I see most mornings
Wrapped in jackets

Puffed muffled and capped
Pumping his bike pedals
Crouched low
For strength or warmth
Up the hill
Toward the middle-school
I have such admiration
For him
Think of the things
He will be able
To tell his lazy kids
   "Back when I
   Was in school…"

2.13
Somewhat cloudy
64/30
Yesterday I missed
Shrove Tuesday pancake
   dinner
Cleaning out the cupboard
Because blood pressure
Went wacky
161/107 freaky
Never that high before
Felt tightness in chest
A little sensation
No pain
While waiting for Theo
To disgorge from school
Theo ill also headache
Tender stomach
Too bad
Wanted to note
The beginning of Lent
Both of us puny
Skipping church
By 9:00 bp down
121/82

I can live with that.

2.14
Valentine's Day
Ash Wednesday
Today
Love day
And
Ash day
Repent day
Ashes to ashes day
Kiss me my love day
I love you forever day
I am a sinner day
17 dead in Florida day
Another white kid
Angry at his high school
Armed with an AR-15
18th school shooting this year
This year This year
[Later corrected, 4th
Can't we trust any Media
To just give us the facts
Man 4th still too many]
And the Republicans
Are running around with their
Prayers and condolences
Tucked into collective asses
Cover your ass day
Fuck you fuck you fuck you
How's that for a poem
NRA?

2.18
We moved to the valley
Six months ago
But we have not driven
To West Virginia yet
So today Colleen and I

Took off west to more
Mountains
We offered to take Theo
To a ski lodge
So he could
Experience a new
Mountain
But he chose not to
Did not wish
To drive two hours
To ski two hours
To drive two hours back
So Colleen and I drove
West to Elkins for lunch
Without him

Kind of disappointed
Middle-class intellectuals
We were
Winter worn
Landscape naked frigid
Trees poverty but no exotic
Oh my god can you believe
People live like that poverty
I think Colleen wanted
Hillbilly Elegy desolation
No Meth or Oxy addicts
In the convenience
Store where I bought
Coffee and cherry drops
Did see strangest thing
Though above us
To the right up high on one
Mountain
Just the top covered
White new snow
I said it's like snow
Was falling only
In that place
The top of the

Mountain
Obviously new snow
And it stopping
Abruptly a white aureole
And down here
In the valley
36 degrees and cloudy

And all of this prelude
To driving home
After lunch on a different
Road out of Elkins
A kind of a loop
The way back through
Mountains
Out of Elkins
Rain well that's lousy
Messy not so pretty
Slosh and splash
And the thwack thwack
Of the wiper blades
Then we begin ascending
And curving
And rain begins to tick
On windshield
Tick tick ticktick
Hey it's beginning to ice
But the car says
The temp is still 34
No problem right
Nothing is sticking
Then we notice
Flakes floating swirling
And still the tick tick
The trees and the ground
All of a sudden are white
This is a little space
Time joke right
At home a snow storm
Comes to us

2018

We watch it arrive
Take joy go out
On the porch
Into the yard
Twirl in it laugh
Here it is we who arrive
It has been snowing
Here a long time
We are the drifters
The outsiders
The roads suddenly
Are white not black
And it's 30 degrees

Nothing to do
But keep going we are
Alone on the road
Which is nothing but
White I look
Behind through the mirror
Am glad to see
Two black tracks
Makes me think the tires
Are cutting through
Shallow snow and up
We go into more
Mountains
Nothing to do
But keep going slowly
Then a truck rushes
Out of a frozen dirt
Driveway bucket
On the front
Snow plow boy am I
Glad to see him
Follow him we think
And do
For ten miles or so
And when there is
A fork in the road

And the road to the right
Higher up a
Mountain
Is pure white no tracks
Has a sign for the town
We planned to go to
Next but the plow goes
Left and I go left
And we go together
(More snow fall
Getting deeper
Now it's 28 degrees)
For five miles until
I see the county limit sign
Oh no the snow plow
Turns into a driveway
Backs out and heads
Back toward us
We are going down the
Mountain
No snow plow in sight
Now and the road is white
The snow is deeper
We are cutting our own tracks
And I can feel how the car
Slides sometimes
Just a little
A couple of cars
Are catching up
I don't care how slow
I have to go
Beside the road
To the right
Is a running creek
Sometimes the road
Sidles up pretty damn
Close to that gulley
Keep 'er straight Lyman
Nothing sudden Lyman
Focus Lyman

Lyman Grant

I don't know whose voice
Is inside my head
But it makes me nervous
There's a slight curve
To the left
I have to make
The little car begins
Its slide/its smooth
Glide to the right
I know suddenly
That I am not in control
The car is a box
Skimming the slick
Sideways as much as forward
And I am trying to remember
All the lessons I never
Needed in Texas
Turn into the slide
But I am sliding toward
The culvert with the creek
Five feet below
Gently tap tap tap
On the break
I am looking at the creek
I am looking at Colleen
I am looking in front
Where I want to go
I turn the wheel that way
Oh god oh god
Really this is where
Our little day leads
Us tipped over
Into the creek really
The car catches two feet
From the drop
My hands shake at
The safety brake
And the gear shift
I can barely make my
Hands do their tasks

And the two cars
Behind us pass us
And travel on

2.22
Just a little note here
The high school students
At Marjory Stoneman Douglas
High School in Parkland
   Florida
Might be changing gun
Rhetoric maybe finally
Enough tears
Enough clinched stomachs
Enough empty desks
Enough ammonia cleaning
Up the bloody classrooms
Enough ghosts brushing
One's shoulders
In mournful hallways

2.27
Watch out
Trump has entered
The building to save you
From the gunman
He has no gun
But the draft dodger
Is rushing the hallways
Empty handed
You believe him
Don't you

2.28
End of the second month
And I still find time
To sit here
And type

In the 40s this morning
And cloudy
Sunny yesterday for once
Usually gray hovers above
Day after day
Everyone says the weather
Is very unusual
Much too warm
We'll pay for it
In March they say
One thing for certain
No matter what
Anyone says
We will see

I should report
However
That I feel as gray
As the sky looks
This is my season
For depression
Always is and has been
Too many poems
About mud and slogging
Through
Just making it
Through the day
That is how I do it
Each day I tell myself
Just make it to the end
Of the day
And then I make it

In a few minutes
I have to stop this
And get ready to go
To my part-time job
Helping grad students write
Seminarians peace and
Justice nurses teachers people

From Macedonia Georgia
South Sudan Tanzania
South Korea, Guadalupe
China good people
Even Americans
It's a good job
I am reading
About Jesus and peace
And the problem
Of church imperialism
About Neoliberalism
About manic depression
And minimum wage
And therapy with horses
And a middle-aged
White guy project manager
Still working to make
Life better after
The great recession
He and I did not hit it off
—no emotion fella
And the emotive poet—
But he's doing
What he has to do
To survive
He's really no different
From the younger activists
Except his privilege
Makes him vulnerable
To losses that others can't lose
Because they don't
Have anything to lose

Anyway I am living
In a gray world for now
Many days I want
To go back home
To Austin
Life here is okay
I guess but

I don't want to be
Here
Time to go
To swim
Then to work

March

3.5
1:15 p.m.
In my office
At work
Waiting for someone
To help
Did some editing
A resume
From a Saudi student
Now I hear
That tick tick tick
On one of my windows
From sleet and rain
iPhone says that it's
42 outside
And that's the high
For the day
Nobody else will come
Today school's out
For March break
But I am still here
For the extra diligent
Looking ahead
Or the panicked
Here right now

Still cloudy

And I think
I'm getting cataracts
In my left eye
Black stringy mass-like
Thing floating shifting
As I read or scan off
In the peripheral
And then depending
Where I look
Sometime in the center
But not when I am
Looking there

It's like having
A quiet friend who isn't
Demanding attention
But always seems to be
There when you turn around
Or look to the side
Oh you're still here
Sometimes when the light
Is right I can see
Almost a black Milky Way
Across my eye the stars
Black dots not lights
Maybe it's like a photo
Negative of the Milky Way
God's funny
I complain about
All the clouds outside
And now there're clouds
Inside my goddamn eye

3.7
Today we learn
That David Dennison
Aka Donald Trump
And Essential Consultants
(whoever they are)
Are being sued by
Peggy Peterson
Aka Stormy Daniels
Aka Stephanie Clifford
Because David did not sign
Their non-disclosure
　agreement
Aka "hush agreement"
Like she did
On 28 October 2016
Just days before the election
And therefore Peggy
Does not have to hush

Even though Peggy hushed
   (sort of)
David never denied
Their farandwee
And hushed up too soon
How do you like your
   blue-eyed
Boy now Mr. Evangelical?

Oh yes and the Vice-President
Used a private server for gov't
   emails
Did I hear the repugnicans
   yelling
Lock him up
I didn't think so

It isn't the deeds that are
   bothersome
Who cares about porn stars
It's the hypocrisy
Behind the red state/faced
   moral outrage
There are no morals
It's only hunger for raw power
Desire for more
They will say anything hurt
Anyone to remain separate
From the people

3.8
Medicare card came today
Except for the fact
That it means that soon
I will be 65
And 6.5/7s to 2/3s of my life
Is in the ditch
I am glad it arrived
Maybe the various bits of
   paper
Are making it to the right
   office
In the right city
In the right state

3.9
A. R. Ammons tells us
   since what one sez or duz
      means nothing, one is
   free to sa & du
   what one likes:
Which means I can continue
To remember this year
As it unfolds to me
And not expect anything
To come from it
Or worry or not
About any plans
In a hundred years
Who is going to remember
   A. R. Ammons anyway
And it won't matter that
For three minutes I fought
Microsoft Word and
Its automatic formatting
Feature and lost
So the only reason A.R.
Ammons was indented above
Had nothing to do with
   meaning
Or intention but because
Because some technician
Somewhere thought it was
A nifty feature
What I say or do means
   nothing
To a nifty thinking technician
And if no one will remember

A. R. Ammons
B. Then they certainly
C. Will not remember
D. Me
E. I mean I have been
F. At this poetry game
G. For many years
H. And have a few friends
I. And a few compliments
J. Along the way
K. But many of us
L. Hell the vast vast majority
M. Of us
N. With our little books of poetry
O. Are going to be forgotten
P. And the nods and the smiles
Q. That we have received
R. In our little readings
S. And the praise
T. That we have received
U. From those we thought better
V. Will be appreciated
W. Will make us warm
X. And boil inside
Y. But all those good feelings
Z. Will leave us
AA. floating into the ether
AB. like steam
AC. until the pot
AD. is empty
AE. you get my point
AF. hell you are not even
AG. reading this
AH. and I don't know how
AI. to get back to my usual
AJ. formatting

Congratulate me
All I had to do
Was keep hitting
Enter
That is the way that we make it
Through life isn't it
Just keep hitting Enter
And keep moving down the page
We are free to do what we like
Most times
Who's going to stop us
No one really cares
Because they are also
Hitting Enter
And moving on themselves
What did you say something
Someone might say
Were you talking to me
I'm sorry but I wasn't listening
I was thinking about my own stuff
Sorry but I have to go

3.12
Snow today
And the calm that falls upon us
Yards and roofs blanketed pure
Bare tree limbs puffed like cotton
Less traffic
Fewer cars
Humming softer slower
Silent white

What if snow
Were red or black
Would we think
Of it differently
Or would we think
Of "white" differently
Would snow provoke anger
Warfare violent sex
The red snow district
Or depression foreboding
And he stepped
Into the dark deadly
And horroring snow
Ok so sue me
I stayed home
From my tutoring job today
Just didn't want to drive
In the snow
I could have
Sure
The roads looked clear
Enough
If slushy
I needed
To catch up
On grading for other classes
I have been having trouble
Making myself sit down
And read
Students' poems
From creative writing class
And read the essays on
American Humanities
Compare and contrast
Works from before and after
World War II
I think it's a good assignment
I'm tired of editing
Tired of explaining a grade

But I sucked up it
As they say
(Now that's
An unpleasant metaphor
Look it up it describes
Swallowing your own vomit)
And read papers
And graded tests
And offered to read through
The grad student work
After hours
(Ain't I a nice guy)
But I also got to sit
At home and watch
The snow fall
Sweet little flakes
Errant and tossed
By the gusts
Silent pure

3.15
Yesterday high low thirties
Yesterday pi day
Yesterday students across the
   nation
Left their classrooms
To gather outside
In memorial
Of the seventeen people killed
In the Florida school
One month ago
Seventeen names
Annunciated loudly
One name one minute
One balloon released
And silence between
Each lonely balloon
Rising a lone name
Fading sound

In circles of grief
And hope
That the end
Of the number
Can be found

My generation has failed
In so many ways

Three weeks ago
Colleen visited
The Appalachian South
   Folklife Center
In Pipestem West Virginia
Volunteering with JMU
   students
To freshen up the paint
In several buildings
She returned with a book for
   me
No Lonesome Road
Selected Prose and Poems
By Don West
(1906-1992)
Christian minister
Small c communist
Labor advocate farmer
Rancher community
Organizer human rights
Activist mountain man
   husband
Father journalist teacher
Poet essayist
He writes about Jesus
In 1967
   Only the man
   who looks like the people
   can lose himself
   among them
   and "the movement"

Often they seem to be
talking to themselves…
proving their "revolutionary
radicalism" by mouthing
many four-letter words
and affecting strange
manners of speech, dress,
and hairstyles that can
only erect barriers of
communication and set
them apart from the people.
It sows confusion,
misunderstanding, and
hinders essential unity
of the people.
And I think
This is how my generation
Of educated hippie
Liberals including me let go
Of the people's hands
Confused and abandoned
Until Roger Ailes sweetly
Placed a remote
In their upturned palms

3.16
Good grief
Sometimes I wonder what
Is the matter with me
Somewhere near Lynchburg
I zigged when I should have
   zagged
Somehow left highway 29
And got on a road going places
I had no intention of going
But I didn't notice
And the GPS telephone had
   gone
Blank and silent

And I am thinking
Man the sun is
In my face
And that means I am
Going west
And I shouldn't be
Going west
And when will the road
Curve back and head south
Finally I see a sign for
Roanoke
And think oh shit
I really am going the wrong
Direction and take the next
Exit to stop at a filling station
For a pee and a tea and look
At my map and confirm
The certainty of my
   misdirection
Lucky me I have exited
Near where highway 43
Heads south and that is
What I do hop on 43
And head south southeast
Where I will catch 29 again
I just love GPS
(he says sarcastically)
So 43 is a two-laner
And rides up and down
And this way and that
A little roller coaster
Of a road not much traffic
But a few cars here and there

Can't tell you everything
I saw on 43
Saw a field crosscut stumps
Like tombstones sad
Grief field and I think
Of a poor man who spends
The last of his money
Just to make his bills
And now what will he do
The next time he needs
To pay some bills
And the field is empty
No green bare nothing
To build with this is America
Today I think we are wasting
Our heritage spending
The principle of our virtues
Then a few more of these
Stricken ex-forests
That are nothing now
A couple of confederate flags
But not as many as American
Flags but what does an
   American
Flag mean to these people
Who live here
Don't know no judgment
They are fellow citizens
The road then begins
A crazy weaving
Up and down and twisting
Around like we are riding
On a serpent's back
It's a writhing road
Watch out hit the brakes
There's the edge pay attention
Hold on thank god
Another car is not coming
At me the other way
I must be riding on the edge
Of mountain and the road
Is following some old trail
Established centuries ago
Native Americans then
Settlers crossed this hill
This way and a river saunters

Down below don't you just
Love the old ways
And the ways they intrude
Upon our straight-lined-
Do-it-our-efficient-ways

I am going to have to come
Back here in the spring
Or summer and see it
When the trees are green
And full I want to know
The names of these trees
A few green junipers
And finally there a clump
Tight and dense of pine
Trees bright green and
Gangly trunks kids
Adolescents someone planted
On the side of this hill
As the road curves away
Knowing someone has to
    reinvest
In nature's bank
Or the accounts will empty
And of course somebody
In a few years will cut all these
Down for profit also
Got to find some way to live
I guess finally I make it
To highway 29
And I call my sister
To tell her
That I will be 45 minutes later
Than I thought I would be

3.17
Lovely day
Pittsboro, NC
Dinner al fresco
With sister brother-in-law
Nephews nieces their spouses
Their children and Theo
Guinness Irish Soda Bread
Corned beef cabbage mashed
Potatoes (with kale) and stories
Fueled by Jameson's
News blackout by choice
Near midnight learn
The day began with
    Andrew McCabe FIRED
    a great day
    for the hard working
    men and women
    of the FBI –
    A great day
    for Democracy.
    Sanctimonious
    James Comey
    was his boss
    and made McCabe
    look like a choirboy.
    He knew all
    about the lies
    and corruption
    going on
    at the highest levels
    of the FBI!
    Donald J. Trump
    @realDonaldTrump
What do the words
"sanctimonious"
And "choirboy" tell us
About the ethics of the
    President
The corrupt despising the
    image
In the mirror
That the incorruptible
Hold up to them

Mirror mirror

3.19
Monday
Harrisonburg
30's cloudy
Blah blah blah
After taking Theo to school
Pulling in toward the garage
At the back of the house
I see a lone robin
(More accurately called
"The American Robin"
(even more accurately called
Turdus migratorius))
In the backyard
Near the little patch
Of daffodils just beginning
To golden
I stop the car
But don't cut the engine
For fear the shift
In noise will flight the bird
It's watchful eye
Twitching knocking
The head tilting
Stick legs balancing
Bold chest and belly
Rust auburn gleam
Racing ten steps and pause
Step step run
Peck at grass dirt peck
Turn over leaves peck
Race three feet
It keeps coming closer
To me I dare not move
Behind the closed window
Breathe just watch no hurry
There is nothing else

You have to do
At this moment
It lifts a leaf
And tosses it aside
Pecks again and again
And it's a worm I can see
That it found a worm
Beige gray and skin glisten
Peck peck peck
Catching the fleshy thing
Mid-body lifting slicing
Through parts fall
The thing raised reduced
In size each time
Peck peck at little parts
Scattered
I look for emotion
Something elation
Satisfaction pride
Caution greed nothing
The long sharp beak doing
What it is good at
That black eye fixing
And re-fixing attention
I know not where
The pause and then the catch
Of the final two inches just
   right
The beak raised to the sky
The throat pulling and
   accepting
Done

I remove my foot from the
   break
Touch the gas and pull
Into the garage
The robin scampers
To the other side of the yard
Then up and away

Time for my breakfast
Instant oatmeal and decaf

3.20-3.21
In the 30s rainy
First day of spring
Vernal Equinox
Sunrise 7:18
Sunset 7:28
Day length 12:10:58
(So why is not
March 17
The equinox
Sunrise 7:23
Sunset 7:24
Day length 12:00:56)
I'm sure
There's some reason
The scientists have
Earth tilt
Or something
But that's not the main thing
I wanted to say
Soon enough
After a good day
With students like
Christopher from Tanzania
Who is writing a sermon
On Isaiah 9:2-7
The temp hit freezing
And now begins
And over night
6-8 inches of snow
No work
Though of course
There is always grading
To be done
So it is not a Sabbath
It is a work day

As much as any day
Just a quiet one
Somehow no one
In the house wants
To speak loudly
In the house when
Everything outside
Is white and
At least for a while
Stopped
Balanced
In a kind of equipoise
Before daylight
Expands
For a while
Greater than darkness
And we hope
That all things will be
Wonderful
Everlasting
Peaceful

3.24
Washington D.C.
9:30 am
The day is warming up
Nicely
Colleen and I
Making our way
From our hotel in Arlington
Uber to Roslyn Station
To L'Enfant Plaza
To Archives
Out to Pennsylvania Ave
For the March for Our Lives
I've never been
To a march before
No Civil Rights protests
No Cambodia/Vietnam

    protests
No Farm Worker's rallies
No El Salvador/Nicaragua
No Nukes
No ERA
No Iraq War I
No Iraq War II
No ….. almost 65
I am more than a little
    Ashamed
I have been a reader
A thinker a navel gazer
A bourgeois want-to-be
Trying to have my liberal
Society and comfy couch
Hard bound books and tequila
    too

But today Colleen and I
Wear our message shirts
We stake out a place
Across from the National
    Archives
Where The Declaration of
    Independence
The Constitution
The Bill of Rights live
Ah don't be tempted
To call this irony
This is our crazy nation
Free speech and gun safety
Argued before the stone
    columns
That home the first
And second amendments
Live today
On your cable favorite channel
By 11:30 we're packed in
No getting out
Just reading signs

Taking photos
Sipping water
Turning cheeks toward the sun
It's all a wash of language
Emotion body crushing
Agora-philia or -phobia
Depending

The NRA is the swamp…drain
    it
Congress: 94% of Americans
    want
Background checks One child
    is worth
More than all the guns on
    earth
No more silence end gun
    violence
What is it with the signs
Part clever ego
Part egoless sincerity
Part superego finger wagging
Part renegade id
Part comedy want-to-bes
The music begins *Rise Up*
    I see it in you
    So we gonna walk it out
    And move mountains
Congress shall make no law
respecting an establishment of
    religion
    But I promise we'll take
    The world to its feet
    And move mountains
or prohibiting the free exercise
    thereof
If only my uterus
could shoot bullets then
it wouldn't need regulation
Only young people speak today

From the stage
Smart move politically
    You can hear the people
    in power shaking
or abridging the freedom
of speech, or of the press;
    I am not afraid to bleed
    If it means
    We'll make a better
    Today tomorrow
Thoughts and prayers are not
    enough
or the right of the people
peaceably to assemble,
Change laws
or change leaders
    Together we will use
    our voices to make sure
    that our schools churches
    movie theaters and concerts
    and our streets become safer
    without having to feel
    like prisons
and to petition the Government
for a redress of grievances.
The only thing easier
to buy
than a gun
is a Republican
    We may not yet have
    reached our glory / But
    we'll surely join the fight /
    And when our children
    tell the story / They'll tell
    the story of tonight,
What is it with Americans and
    guns
I'd rather have
A Kinder Egg
Than a gun
If teachers start packing
    heat
are they going to arm
our pastors ministers and
    rabbis
are they going to arm
the guy taking tickets
at the movie theater
are they going to arm
the person wearing
the Mickey Mouse
costume at Disney
Don't protect guns protect us
A well-regulated Militia,
being necessary
to the security of a free State,
    The people demand
    a law banning the sale
    of assault weapons
    The people demand
    the prohibition
    of high capacity magazines
    The people demand
    universal background
    checks
    Stand with us or beware
    The voters are coming
the right of the people
to keep and bear Arms,
shall not be infringed.
The scariest things in a school
should be my grades
If you need a machine gun to
hunt you suck at it
    Go on and try
    to tear me down
    I will be rising
    from the ground
Enough is enough
    I am here to acknowledge

and represent
the African American girls
whose stories
don't make the front page
of every national newspaper,
whose stories
don't lead
on the evening news
Don't panic....Organize
We are coming for you in
    November
    Today is the beginning
    of a bright new future
    for this country

Because I am old
And cannot stand
For long
I have brought
My cane chair
And am up and down
Sitting and standing
And when I am sitting
I can see
Only the backs
And quarter-turned faces
Of my fellow citizens
Tears nods raised fists
Closed mournful eyes
Bowed heads proud
Clinched jaws
And teenage girls
Behind me
Keep bumping shoving
Me so they can see
The screens
That have been placed
For everyone
Along Pennsylvania Ave
There are hundreds

Of thousands of us
Blocks and blocks
Filled with people
Of all ages
Praying for the killing
To stop
    Raise a glass
    To freedom
    Something they can
    Never take away

Most of us cannot see
The stage
Blocks and blocks
Away
We are packed
Into our shoulder
To shoulder worlds
Watching speeches
Reading signs
Smiling at each other
And listening
To singers
The teenage girls
Scream when Demi
Lovato takes the stage
And lean over me
As I sit to get better sight
Of her on the screen
They sing along
Into my ears
The most heartbreaking
Voices passionate yearning
Feeling all the feels
    You can take everything I have
    You can break everything I am
    Like I'm made of glass
    Like I'm made of paper
I cannot be angry
That my body

Is in their way
We are here together
For the same reason
Our hearts are breaking
For all the young people
Who have been shot
For this country
Whose soul is so violent
And violated
For all the young people
Who must go to school
Next week and not know
If the next shooter
Will not rush their halls
And classroom
And murder their friends
Gun down the favorite
Loving teacher who stands
In the way of the shooter
Why won't
The government
Protect them
I have failed them
Let these girls sing
Let them have all the space
They need
   It has been six minutes
   And twenty seconds
   The shooter has ceased
   Shooting and will soon
   Abandon his rifle
   Blend in with the students
   As they escape
   And walk free
   For an hour before arrest
   Fight for your lives before
   It is someone else's job
My outrage cannot fit on this
   sign

3.31
Saturday Birmingham
6:00 a.m. 43 degrees
What the hell
Am I doing up
After a couple of vivid
Serious dreams
I woke up feeling
Anxious
Some tightness in the chest
Feeling like I was not
Getting enough oxygen
The right nostril sinus
Clogged feeling I needed
To focus on remembering
To breathe more deeply/
Fully am I about to have
A heart attack or panic
Attack that's what I was thinking
Calm yourself down boy
Now I am downstairs
Eating a breakfast
At the Comfort Inn
(very bizarre eggs
Microwaved to look
Like fried eggs but
Stare at me like big yellow eyes
Wake up we are looking
At you boy)
The orange juice
Made me feel better
Was my blood sugar low
I need to get cup of decaf
And go back to the room
I promised I would read
A friend's manuscript
And I am running a day or two
Late Colleen is going
To a park to walk the dog
Now's the time

To get some work done

Very good day
I think
Just hanging with the middle
  son
That's why we are here
In Birmingham
To visit Jacob at college
He's back from his spring
  break
Theo is finishing his spring
  break
Colleen and I have days off
Because of Easter
Walked around the
  Birmingham
Art Museum lovely museum
Colleen brought us here
To look at the "Third Space"
Exhibit—"The Global South"
Basically the extending
  relationships
Of racism exacted and
  experienced
After that because of my
  humanities
Class I wandered over
To Native American art
Which I admit "I don't
Quite get" whatever that might
  mean
Here's an example I can admire
With different levels of interest
Totems baskets blankets
  pottery
Shaman headdresses but then
I spot two works by Edmonia
  Lewis
And I am in awe This is Beauty
But then I have to ask myself
Which came first
Has my intellectual training
Determined my aesthetic
  sensibility
Or are we who we are
And eventually find the beauty
That naturally will speak to us
You know that feeling don't you
You live your life day to day
And then one day you hear
A piece of music see a painting
A flower a landscape a person
And you feel
You open up
You are for a moment being
The person you always
Didn't know but yearned to be
You think it is all pre-intellectual
You love it because you do
Not because someone with
  degrees
Told you too
And then you learn the professors
Love it too

April

4.1
Easter
He is risen
He is risen indeed
Up early
Breakfast with Jacob
At The Original Pancake
   House
(I don't know
What's so original
About this one
There must be over
A hundred of them
National-wide
But the original original
Pancake House
In Portland is
As old as I will be
In three days
Is there any meaning in that)
Then ten hours on the road
Back home
Good visit I miss Jacob
Being in the house
With us
Every day
But the kids have to grow up
And he's doing
A fine job of that

One thing I thought about
Was two things/places
177 Ross Drive
324 Redwood St
Two houses I lived in
In Birmingham
From 1953-1964
Childhood homes
We drove by yesterday
Just to see
Both a little run down
Neither the best or worst
House on the block
I stood in the street
At both houses
To take photos
To send to my sisters
But I wonder why
This is a schizoid exercise
I return to re-capture
Memories I guess
Beautiful mossy fairyland
In a nearby creek
Exciting rock climbing
On huge (in memory)
   outcroppings
An Easter rock fight
With neighborhood kids
Bloody forehead and
   emergency room
Another time
Peeing in my pants
Down the block
Because I was told to come
   home
Now my parents are angry
A roller skate cart
God the noise of that
My mother taking my photo
Because I look like what she
   thinks
Huck Finn would look like
Timing ourselves walking
   home
From elementary school
During the Cuban missile
   crises
To see if we could make it
   home
Before the big one hits

Throwing a rubber ball against
The tall backyard wall
Practicing grounders and
Long outfield flies
Saturday night popcorn
Testing my gun drawing
Against Matt Dillon

This is a compulsion
Sort of
Where do these memories
Reside
Do I even want them
To be enlivened
These places and that being
That I am overlapping
Containers of time
Here is the big question
For me
Standing in the street
While other people are
Inside with their own ghosts
Their own past lives/
Multiple selves
Walking around talking
To each other
And who knows
Maybe to my ghosts also
And my sister's and parent's
 ghosts
They bump into each other
In a crowded door frame
And say are you still here
Why haven't you left yet
There is my father
At the brick barbecue pits
He built at each house
It's a sunny Saturday
Before Easter Sunday
And the other people's

2010 memory ghost
Looks out the window
And says to no one in
 particular
There's that guy again
Broiling the T-bones
Back in 1963 and his son
Playing with the plastic
Civil War soldiers making
The South win again
The smoke rises in the breeze
But here's the big question
I am going to say it this time
Would I want my entire life
To have been lived
Would I want all my ghosts
In this town in one of these
 houses
Who would that ghost be
Those ghosts
And if I don't want to be
That ghost
Those ghosts
Why am I standing in the
 street
Wondering what is going on
 inside
Why not mean it
When we say good-bye

Inside there is a mother yelling
At her son she has a leather
Belt doubled it up in her fists
And is thwacking the ten-year
 old boy
This time he grabs the belt
 from her
And tells her it is time
That she stops whipping him
Inside the ghosts are still

52   *Lyman Grant*

staring
At each other
But this mother will not
Beat this boy again
And you know what prompted
The argument that prompted
The beating it was all about
Pancakes
How the boy wanted to eat
The dinner the mother had
   prepared
That night he didn't want
   syrup
She thought that was weird
Pancakes

4.2
Three long days
Too busy for Trump
And today he is back
Lying about Jeff Bezos
Lying about DACA
Lying about Shulkin
Quitting cabinet post
And now Sinclair News
Makes its anchors repeat
The same fake news mantra
Is this how fascism
Takes over a country

4.4
Let me mention
The mixed feelings
Of having a birthday
That shares the date
When Martin Luther King Jr
Was killed
I turned

Fifteen that day and
Although the nation
Has progressed a bit
We still have so far to go
Last weekend
Sitting in the Costco
Parking lot in Birmingham
Alabama with my fifteen-year-
Old son Theo we heard
A white man say "nigger"
In the same way I heard it
Used in Birmingham
When I lived there
In the early 60's
So much time
Will Theo be 65
And still hear
That hateful ignorant slur
My birthday wish
Is that he will not
Now I will take a breath
And maybe on another day
I will say something
Less mournful to honor
The more joyful aspects
Of this day
This evening
At 7:05 Eastern Standard
   Time
At Eastern Mennonite
   University
The time when news
Of Dr. King's assassination
Was announced on the East
   Coast
This evening
After working with students
From Tanzania Iran
South Sudan I
Sat on a bench and watched

Students and teachers
Hold hands say prayers
And remember Dr. King
With 39 chimes
Of the campus church bell
One for each year
Of his great life

4.9
Good grief
30 degrees
Ash flecks of snow
What is this
Back in Texas
When my students and I
Would read "The Waste Land"
I would joke about April
Being the cruelest month
In Texas it was
75 degrees with clear skies
Bright caressing sun
Bluebonnets along every
   highway
Paintbrush Indian blanket
   Mexican hat
Eliot's awakening tubers
Were our February
Here in Virginia will I ever
Get used to this long yawn
Of winter awakening
Months it takes
Who could desire to lift
The blanket of domestic
Hibernation to step
Onto the chill floor
Of daily responsibility
Ignore the god awful
Jangle coin temptation
Of the punch clock wage

How can we miss
What we never had

4.10
Donald J. Trump's reaction
To news that FBI raided
Offices of his personal lawyer
Michael D. Cohen:
   So, I just heard that they
      broke
   in to the office of one
   of my personal attorneys,
   a good man,
   on what we all stand for.

So when I saw this
and when I heard it —
I heard it like you did —
I said that is really now
in a whole new level
of unfairness.
I saw one of the reporters
who is not necessarily a fan
of mine, not necessarily
very good to me,
he said in effect
that this is ridiculous,
this is now getting
   ridiculous.

They found no collusion
whatsoever with Russia,
the reason they found it
is there was no collusion
at all.
No collusion.

This is the most biased
group of people,

these people have
the biggest conflicts
of interest I've ever seen.

They're not looking
at all of the things
that happened
that everybody
is very angry about,

They only keep looking at
   us.
So they find no collusion,
and then they go from there
and they say, "Well,
let's keep going,"
and they raid an office
of a personal attorney
early in the morning
and I think it's a disgrace.

It's a disgrace.
I've been president now
for what seems like
a lengthy period of time.

Our economy is incredible.
The stock market dropped
a lot today
as soon as they heard the
   noise
of, you know,
this nonsense
that's going on.
It dropped a lot.
It was up —
way up —
and then it dropped
quite a bit at the end,
a lot.

But that we have to go
through that,
we've had that hanging
over us now
from the very,
very beginning
and yet the other side,
they don't even bother
looking.

Lies under oath,
all over the place,
emails that are knocked out,
that are acid-washed
and deleted,
nobody's ever seen —
33,000 emails are deleted
after getting a subpoena
from Congress,
and nobody bothers
looking at that.

With all of that being said,
we are here
to discuss Syria tonight.
We're the greatest fighting
   force
anywhere in the world.

These gentlemen and ladies
are incredible people.
Incredible talent,
and we're making a decision
as to what we do
with respect
to the horrible attack
that was made near
   Damascus,
and it will be met,

and it will be met
forcefully.

We had $700 billion
just approved,
which was the reason
I went along with that
    budget,
because we had to fix
our military.

General Mattis would tell
    you
that above anybody,
we had to fix
our military
and right now we're in a big
process of doing that,
$700 billion
and then $716 billion next
    year.

So we're going to make
a decision
tonight
or very shortly thereafter
and you'll be hearing
the decision.
Especially when we're able
    to,
because of the power
of the United States,
because of the power
of our country,
we're able to stop it.

I want to thank
Ambassador John Bolton
for joining us.
Interesting day,

he picked today
as his first day.
So, generals, I think
he picked the right day.
But certainly you're going
to find it very exciting

Well, I think
it's a disgrace,
what's going on.
And many people have said
you should fire him.

We'll see what happens.
But I think
it's really a sad situation
when you look
at what happened.

Again, they found nothing
and in finding nothing,
that's a big statement.

I fired Comey,
well, I turned out
to do the right thing
because you look
at all of the things
that he's done
and the lies
and you look
at what's gone on
at the F.B.I.
with the insurance policy
and all of the things
that happened,
turned out I did
the right thing.

So we'll see

what happens.
I think
it's disgraceful
and so does a lot
of other people.
This is a pure and simple
witch hunt.
Thank you
   very much.
Thank you.
Thank you.
Thank you.
Thank you all
   very much.
Thank you.

So people now say
That Trump is setting
The stage to fire
One or all
Sessions
Rosenstein
Mueller
I think the question
Is less
What will Trump do
It's what will we do
When he does
How does one know
How does one acknowledge
When the Fascist state
Has begun

4.11
40 degree morning
7:20 am
Taking Theo to school
Cardinal
The color of pasta sauce

Walking the fence top
Weather-worn gray
Splintered and chipped
Singing
Just singing
And then
Away

4.13
Beautiful bright day
At home
In study
Editing power point
On educational technology
By a grad student from Saudi
   Arabia
Colleen stops by
With two friends from JMU
Eva and Joann visiting scholars
From China
We talk about poetry
Li Po whom they called Li Bai
Show them my poems
Translated to Chinese
In Schroeder's anthology

Today
Is my father's birthday
He would be 107
He has been dead
30 years
Don't know what
I think of that
Will I still be alive
In 12 years
His age when he died
Don't know what
I think about him
My poems entangle him

In anger and grief
It's the net I toss
Over him when he emerges
From the depths
Of memory
Like an ancient catfish
Ugly slime coated
Wary and wise

Why have I let my father
Become the container
For the sharp and rusty
Scraps of my life
That dirty cobwebbed
Jar in the garage filled
With old bent nails
   unmatched
Nuts and bolts burnt fuses
   broken
Hinges cup shards tacks
Dried pens and loose blades
Tokens of failure and wrath
The thing that I call Father
Is stored half inside and half
Outside the house
While inside the house
I hum songs by Hoagy
Carmichael and Glenn Miller
Watch baseball read history
   love
These United States plan
A road trip love my wife
And sons work pay for food
And college crack a joke
About some poor schmuck
These too are "Father" but
These I call "myself"

At Rose Mountain three years
Ago I said it was time to let

My father back into the house
This is what I think I am
   learning
These days how we invite
The whole person inside the
   house
All the way inside to the
   dinner
Table to share meals to listen
And to love even when he
Says things we cannot agree
   with
He might say "nigger" he
   might
Say that I am lazy and will
   never
Amount to anything he might
   say
I have not respected him he
Might say that something's
   wrong
With me that I enjoy helping
"Foreigners" learn English
He might say something about
"Mexicans" and "homos" he
   might

Or maybe he might not
A lot has happened in thirty
   years
I am not the same person why
Would I think that he would
   be
Why wouldn't he think
   differently
Now so thanks
Okay we will still pass
The lentils and rice the green
   salad
Iced tea and apple pie I can

Listen I can tell him where I
    disagree
I can thank him for all the
    gifts
And love he has given me my
    sisters
Our husbands and wives our
    children
Our children's children let's
    have a beer
Let's watch a game let's go
    outside
And toss the ball around
Theo has his glove I have mine
    and
Yes I still have his in the attic
It's a beautiful day we'll
Toss the ball around
Like old times before time
Got away from us

4.14
From Donald J. Trump
    A perfectly executed strike
    Last night
    Thank you
    To France
    And the United Kingdom
    For their wisdom
    And the power
    Of their fine Military
    Could not have had
    A better result
    Mission Accomplished
    @realDonaldTrump
How am I supposed
To have an opinion
Or a reasoned judgment
About such matters

This is a game
Played at the highest levels
By the most suspect people
What kinds of lies
Preceded such decisions
What kind of war
Will follow
What kind of war
Would follow
If we yes we
I am part of this
Did nothing
People are dying
And I should care
About that
Are we perpetuating
Death
Or preventing
Death
My impotence
And my culpability
Were determined long ago
When I decided to be
An English teacher
And poet
And not a rich man
And politician
In a world of lies
And secrets
How am I to know
The truth of this

4.16
Yesterday
Lovely warm morning
Then evening thunder storms
And temp falls
Feeling kind of gloomy
All day

It could be the bombing
It could be the Trump/
Comey battle of words
It could be I wish I had friends
Here in Harrisonburg
It could be so many things
My general malaise
My constant sense of failure
Things that have passed
My vision reading *Rassalas*
Reading Bloom on Johnson
Pacino as Paterno *Wonder
Woman* Elvis's final years
Elton John Prine
Renbourn *The Circus
Homeland* 30 Powerpoints
By students on various
   Americans
Poems by students in another
   class
Farmer's Market swim at JMU
   pool
Because I just seem
To get fatter and fatter
The Nats and the Orioles
Both losing but hey
Carrie Underwood's face looks
Pretty good that's good news
And today at least
Did not get worse

4.17
Morning
33 degrees cloudy
This chill morning
The narcissus spreads
Its white wings wide
In showy display
Of its golden cupped corona
The clinched red fisted tulip
Awaits the touch
Of a reluctant spring
The climbing rose
Hangs on uninterested
And the robin turns over
Last year's leaves
His black-eye watches
While the man
In his dirty housecoat
Hurries to retrieve
The town's thin newspaper
Nods to the student
Wrapped in sweaters
Scarves gloves head down
Against the wind
Worried about today's test
Not noticing a thing

4.19
Last night
At EMU
I sat with Colleen
And hundreds of students
And faculty listening
To Fania Davis
Talk about race racism
Genocide and restorative
   justice
It was my idea for Colleen
And me to attend but
I will not pretend
I take in these words
Her words
Spoken by her
To me
Or so it seemed
Easily willingly graciously

4.20
And then
Last night
I sat with Colleen
At Massanutten Regional
    Library
In Harrisonburg
With 30 citizens
Or so listening
To a professor
Talk about memory
And history
Of James Madison University
Founded in 1908
As a normal
Critique of surveillance
Of young girls
Of unrecognized rebellions
Sneaking out at night
Of accepted racist practices
Minstrel blackface
By the young women
And the faculty and
    administration
Of unwritten and suppressed
History of African American
Lives lived on the campus
Gardeners cooks laundresses
Met a man
Who pushed for the town
To rename a street
Named for a Confederate
General as MLK Way
(and won)
Met another man
Who is recovering African
American history in
Harrisonburg and who
Considers Fania Davis his
    mentor

Now I stop typing
And get dressed to attend
A chapel service at EMU
To be led by Dr. Davis

Oh yes Earth Day
I guess I should think
About that
But I don't really

4.21
Beautiful day
40s-60s
Sun
Farmer's Market in morning
With Colleen
Spinach pak choi
Lettuce onions
Blackberry jam
River Park in Bridgewater
In afternoon
Porch swing in full sun
Colleen and I
Kicking legs against air
For rise and return
Mallards drift on river
Above dam
Diving tail feathers high
Orange feet frantic
Resisting the water
A fisherman's quick wrist
And the line whirring
In a flat S and laying out
Upon the water
The spinning return
Our bodies as machines
Levers hinges fulcrums
Weights

4.22
Mahler's 2nd
At JMU
With its orchestra
And chorus
And orchestra and chorus
Of the Governor's School for
    Arts
Just college and high school
    kids
And their teachers
What an ordeal this symphony
    is
To listen to it
Is to churn in sentimentality
Dread chaos hope anxiety
Unfulfilled searching sighs
And growls never ending
    tumult
Yearning joy timpani harp
Trombone oboe cello and voice
Rise again yes rise again
And again and again
And fall and fall
And rise again
In our greatest pain angels
Turn away but we will rise
Find our own wings
We will find our home
In the universe
We will rest in the light
Of a never-ending dawn
The ovation stands and
A sweet pimple blotched
Girl with stringy blonde hair
Presses her violin to her chest
Tears soaking her smile
A joy
And the ever-present
Sometimes misplaced

Gift

4.25
Die Schone Mullerin
At EMU
In the Martin Chapel
Performed by two
JMU professors
As overwhelming as Mahler
In its own way
An hour of dread and vanished
    love
A maiden won and lost
A brook longing in watery
    song
Piano rushing and waterfalling
Pausing halting stepping softly
Flowers bloom and the moon
Maddens into frenzy
What kind of man
Wins the heart of a simple
Woman can I ask these days
The poet loses again
To the man with a gun
Blasting through the woods
The NRA can say
They told us so
A gentle romanticism
Lay bleeding on the green
Gute ruh rest well
The hunting horn echoes
Thunder rumbles

4.26
Warming but raining
Trump on Fox and Friends
Volleys a jumble of words
Does it matter what order

We listen to them in
A horrible thing
And yet I've accomplished
With all of this going on
More than any president
In the first year in our history
You know I'm very busy
To be running out looking
For presents OK
But I got her a beautiful card
It's a big monster
And some beautiful flowers
So there's no collusion
Whatsoever
I've taken the position
And I don't have to
Take this position
And maybe I'll change
That I will not be involved
I will wait until this is over
He's got a tremendous heart
I did a great thing
For the American people
By firing him

We really accomplished a lot
More than anybody knows
You'll be seeing what we
Accomplished
I would give myself an A+
You can ask President Putin
About that
The nuclear war
Would have happened
I better not get into that
Because I may get in trouble
Maybe I didn't
Get her so much
There's been nobody

Hilliary Clinton Jim Jordan
Mark Meadows and Matt
Gaetz DeSantis and so
Many
Corey Lewandowski
Diamond and Silk Doc
Ronny Jon Tester
Democrats
Russians Michael Cohen
Justice Department Stormy
Daniels Kanye Electoral
College France VA Little
Rocket Man FBI CNN
NBC Republicans
Anderson
Cooper Hillary Clinton
Justice
Department I have many
Many just so you understand
I have many attorneys
I have attorneys sadly
I have so many attorneys
You wouldn't even believe it
All they do
Is scream Death
To America,
Death to America
But I'm not involved
And I'm not involved
And I've been told
I'm not involved
I don't watch things now
There is no collusion
With me

4.28
Virginia Institute of
    Blacksmithing
Waynesboro

Beautiful bright sun
70 degrees
Inside most of day
While Theo forges
Hammer striking
Radiating metal
Red and yellow
Like an angry animal's claw
He is attentive to the fire
To make more malleable
Smudged faced Vulcan
Blistering his hands
I read a book
On history of ethics
Furies into Eumenides
Thrasymachus' unanswered
Challenge
What if he simply
Uses his power
And names that justice
Theo taps and pounds
His first spear tip

May

5.3
Standing at the second-story
Window looking east
The sun hinting behind
The neighboring houses
I yearn again to be awed
Inhabited
The film of my humanity
Cleaned wiped away
So that Your light
Can pierce me
To the kernel
And burst outward
So that I see
With Your illumination
Imbued
With Your charity
These trembling leaves
Spring greened
In unexplainable hope

I am owned
Down to my nuclei
By doubt

5.5
Today
Lovely day
Low 70s sunny

Yesterday
High 80s
And humid
In the evening
Colleen and I strolled
Around downtown
   Harrisonburg
For this month's version
Of First Friday

"Chocolate Walk"
An event to raise money
For a child advocacy group
   "1 in 3 women and 1 in 5
      men
   Are sexually assaulted
   Before the age of 18"
Colleen met up with three
Young women from
Her program at JMU
You do the math

Today
Fine drive to Williamsburg
For the annual meeting
Of the Poetry Society of
   Virginia
An afternoon of poetry
Pretty good poetry
In fact
Mostly gray as these groups
Usually turn out to be
But a good mix of serious
Page poets lyrical memories
Of families in tidewaters
Video projects and a street
   poet
Coffee house poets
Sestinas and spoken word
Crickets and child abuse
Had to go all the way
To Williamsburg
To find a poet
From Harrisonburg
But I done it
Maybe I have a new poet
   friend
Someone in my local life
Who believes that words
Are dreams

And dreams converse with
Boring daily life
And daily life and incidents
Of beauty and terror
Dance beneath the dull
  language
Of one's day-to-day duty

After poetry
We head to Merchants Square
Abutting Colonial
  Williamsburg
The Cheese Shop
(Thank goodness
There's no -pe
Suffixing this shop
No olde world kitsch here)
We find a table outside
Bottle of Barbourville
  Vineyards
Cabernet Franc
Soft and hard cheeses
A jar of pepper jelly
Slices of baguette
And watch the American
  parade
Next to us a middle-aged
  blonde
Dressed in various shades of
  coral
Sits expectantly with her
  packages
From the Scotland House
Holding her tiny fright of a
  dog
A wild haired toddler avoids
Her mother's frustrated hands
A skinny South Asian woman
Severe face and jeans binding
A non-existent ass

Pulls a distracted five-year old
With the stick of her arm
A chubby Hispanic couple
(Chubby like me)
One child in a stroller
Two leading
Smile and joke with each other
Animate appreciation
Of being here now
A late-twenties couple
Blonde pony-tail frown
Pushing double stroller
Pause and examine
The posted menu
Her broad chested man
(Former soldier?)
Stands five feet behind sullen
They mumble past each other
And move on
Our neighbor in coral is joined
By a man with bags of
  sandwiches
Middle-aged couples in suits
And dresses and gold dangles
Stroll with their college-aged
Sons and daughters
And enter what must be a finer
Restaurant across the
  courtyard
(Graduation weekend?
From William and Mary)
The screaming wild-haired
  toddler
Returns clasped in her father's
  arms
(At least we hope it's her dad)
 As he strides through the
  crowd
College girls in heels wobble
  by

Pencil skirts and blouses
Without backs
Two fifties couples
Gray and ash blonde
Pale as fading dogwood
    blossoms
Women dismiss the menu
And tell secrets
Men talk about Princeton
I ponder the thin woman's face
Lines refusing her powder
Every edge eyes lips nostrils
Tug heavily in disappointment
They head across the way
To a bar
Then return thirty minutes
    later
The coral woman leaves
For more shopping
And her companion holds
The half handful of their dog
Whiskers drooping and
    topknot
Tufted with a pink bow
He cups water in his hand
And offers it to the rat
Lets the varmint lick
Whatever wetness remains
A young man in a white suit
Twirling a wooden crookneck
Cane flows through the crowd
His chest and head erect
And still
Blowing smoothly
Like a breeze
And is gone
And emptiness fills
The couple with the twins
Returns passing the other way
Pauses again to peruse the
    menu
She leads
He pushes the stroller
When they speak
They might hear each other
This time
The man with the ribboned yip
Leaves and
The leashed hairball
Scurries into the crowd
Colleen tells me
If I ever get a dog like that
She will leave me

5.9
And then
The continuing Giuliani
    craziness
Trump backing out
Of treaty with Iran and our
    Allies
Michael Cohen's slush fund
Paid for by AT&T Novatis
And Viktor Vekselberg
And then North Korea frees
Three American prisoners
While CIA waterboarder
Gina Haspel oaths
Her way to chief
Quibbles nuances
Of torture and immorality
    My parents raised me
    To know right from wrong
And the sun has not yet
Reached its zenith today

5.11
Friday

Beautiful beautiful day
Sunny mid-80s
Colleen's Mother's Day request
A trip to Montpelier
Founding Father
James Madison's
Home until death
Did him part from Dolley
In 1836
And the home
Of over 100 slaves
Then after many owners
Home to Marion duPont Scott
And her thorough-bred
And steeplechase horses
Now in national trust

You might ask
Why would Colleen wish
To visit a slave owning
President's house
For Mother's Day
The Tuscan portico
The old brick
The stunning view
From the upstairs window
Where Madison sat
In his father's library
In 1787
Studying the history
Of governmental structure
Because the Articles of
    Confederation
Were grossly inadequate
And it all leading to
The Constitution
Sure
None of that

Montpelier

Leads many national
    institutions
In truth telling
About the institution
Of slavery
And the lives and
    contributions
Of enslaved peoples
That is what Colleen
Wanted to see
The name of the permanent
    exhibit
"A mere distinction of colour"
Pulled from a 6 June 1787
Speech/debate at
the Federal Convention
    We have seen
    the mere distinction
    of colour
    made in the most
        enlightened
    period of time,
    a ground
    of the most oppressive
    dominion
    ever exercised
    by man over man

I hobbled around
With my cane chair
Plopped on whatever chairs
Or benches available
On the tour
While the docent gingerly
Room by room
Laid the factual trail
That Madison never intended
To architect a democracy
Nation states
Decentralized authority

Of the wealthy
Garnering power
Avoiding taxes
For Enlightened rule
 The lesson we are to draw
  from the whole
 is that where a majority
 are united
 by a common sentiment,
 and have an opportunity,
 the rights of the minor
  party
 become insecure.
 In a Republican Govt.
 the Majority if united
 have always an opportunity.
 The only remedy is to
  enlarge
 the sphere, & thereby
 divide the community
 into so great a number
 of interests & parties,
 that in the 1st. place
 a majority will not be likely
 at the same moment
 to have a common interest
 separate from
 that of the whole
 or of the minority;
 and in the 2d. place,
 that in case they shd.
 have such an interest,
 they may not be apt
 to unite
 in the pursuit of it.
 It was incumbent on us
 then to try this remedy,
 and with that view
 to frame a republican
  system

on such a scale
& in such a form
as will controul
all the evils
wch. have been experienced

Colleen patient
Then freed for a longer
 walking
Tour of grounds
Where the enslaved lived
And worked
In 1860 80%
of American exports
were produced
by the enslaved
Raised families
Some learning to read
And write
Archeologists now finding
Buttons and pins
Quartz in the corners
Of rediscovered foundations
Of chinked and daubed
Field cabins
Of wood framed one rooms
For house slaved
Overseen from mansion's
Southern wing
We know their names/
Names they were assigned
 Esther Thom Nancy John
 Charlotte Taby Daingerfield
 Stephen Elijah Polly Aleck
 Sukey Fanny Nany Betty
 Abraham Anthony Ailsey
  Payne
 Ellen Stewart George
  Gilmore
 Sarah Stewart Rebecca

       Walker
    Benjamin McDaniel
    Paul Jennings
    Charity
Remembered as property
Remembered as labor
Remembered as family
Remembered as ancestors
Remembered as Americans
Remembered beneath and by
A two-hundred-year-old
Walnut tree
Roots reaching
Into the ruins
Of the once living
Of the once lost and hidden
The trunk ever-rising
The branches ever-witnessing
And uncovering
Recovering
Unrecovering
Is there a word
Balancing/rebalancing
Repenting

5.13
Can't let them go
Still remembering
Two days later
Two editorials
In the local paper
Last Friday
Humored by George Will's
Below the fold
Assessment of how
    The oleaginous
    Mike Pence
    with his talent
    for toadyism
and appetite
for obsequiousness
could… become
America's
most repulsive
public figure
Titled
    "Pence Is a Model
    Of Governing
    By Groveling"
Above the fold
Laura Hollis'
    "The Tyranny
    of the Elites"
Grabs two confessional
Essays by two repentant
Northeastern privileged
Ivy Leaguers
From 2008 and 2012
All to finally diminish
Criticism of Donald Trump
    Their collective
    temper tantrum
    when the American
    electorate decided
    to think for themselves
    —and their leviathan efforts
    to undo the election results
    —are example of what
        happens
    when the disaffected elites
    don't get their way.
Somehow a man who can't talk
To a plumber
And a frat boy at Dartmouth
Who swam in a kiddy pool
Of vomit piss and shit
Become emblematic
Of Hillary Clinton John Kerry
Barack Obama Robert Mueller

And somehow Mark
    Zukerberg
Big stretch
If you ask me

Hollis' class envy
Emerges
From the froth
Of her intellectual dishonesty
Like a great white
Indiscriminate teeth
Eager for the flesh
Of bigger fish

She might be right
About a privileged few
She is certainly wrong
About Trump

I have two reactions
First when Hollis says
    One can only imagine
    what he would say
    about Donald Trump—
    or the 63 million people
    who voted for him
I wonder what she thinks
Of the 66 million who did not
There must be
So many elites
Even those who did not attend
The Ivies
Second Hollis forgets
That Madison and Hamilton
Had her number centuries ago
The Republic will resist
And reform the whims
Of a jealous
And careless mob
Led by people

Like Joe Arpaio
Whom Trump pardoned
And Pence praises
One does not need imagine
What George Will
An Ivy
Thinks
    Trump is what he is,
    a floundering, inarticulate
    jumble of gnawing
    insecurities
    and not-at-all
    compensating vanities,
    which is pathetic.
    Pence is what he has
    chosen to be,
    which is horrifying

Oh yes
Happy Mother's Day
A flowering basket
Hanging pastels on the porch
Chocolates and tea towels
Cards from her boys
High 80's
Air conditioning switched on
In the warming afternoon
Some grading and writing
Theo and I play catch
In the back yard
We all go out for Thai
With Colleen's cousin
And now a glass of Pendleton
As I type this
The burn and grace
Of bourbon
Good night

5.14

Dear Vice Chairman
Mark Warner
I appreciate the
   opportunity...
I have learned the hard
   lessons...
With regard
To the former
   rendition...
Detention and
   interrogation...
To amplify my position...
It was a mistake...
I won't condemn...
The program did damage...
With the benefit
Of hindsight...
To our officers...
And our standing
In the world...
I have noted...
Enhanced interrogation...
Valuable intelligence...
Is not the CIA...
The United States
Must be an example...
I support that...
Oversight committee...
Who make decisions
That can't be made public...
Should have undertaken...
For your thoughtful
Consideration...
I refuse to undertake...
Thank you...
Sincerely
   Gina Haspel
She will be approved
Even as she blamed
The Senate

For her sins

5.15
I am thinking
About a photograph
Of my mother
My two sisters
And me
In northern Michigan
One summer
Maybe '55 or '56
We are standing
Against a wooden fence
Two parallel sets of rails
Round smooth stripped of
   bark
One rung nestled in gashes
Six inches above the ground
The other
Capping the notch poles
At my short mother's shoulder
   blades

The way the photograph
Is composed
You would think the fence
Is tall huge
Until you notice
How short the woman is
And how young the children
   are
My sisters' chests still flat
Stand close to my mother
Feet on the bottom rail
And loom a head taller
Diane the good daughter
In her white blouse
Round collar buttoned
To the neck

Barbara sweater tied
Around her waist
Like a saddle
On a restless pony
And me burr hair cut
Standing apart from the women
Feet on bottom rail
Arms stretched behind
On top rail
Like wings
Like a dove
Or a fledgling hawk
Who can tell yet
We all stare at my father
Snapping the camera

And now outside the photo
Where my father stood
Looking at us
I watch my mother
Early thirties
The warnings of grey
Dark patterned skirt
Blowing in the breeze
From behind us
White short sleeved blouse
Wrinkled
The tails of her scarf
Winding
A tired gypsy
She holds a dark jacket
In her left arm
In the far background
Through tall grass and brush
I can see a house
And four windows
A steeple rises nearby
We are on vacation
But we look

Like we are on the run
We've crossed one border
Hurry
We have a way to go
Before night fall

5.16
I am writing so much lately
I should let some days pass
Be more selective
You don't want to read
All this

But this morning
7:33
Returning home
From taking Theo to school
Stopped at the red light
At Bruce and Liberty
Two mallards crossing
The intersection
Diagonally
In front of me
The hen leading
Drab mottled buff and brown
The drake waddling behind
His iridescent head
Like Chrome Tourmaline
Unheeding

I watch
And fret as cars
Rush by
A blue Toyota white
F-150 black Lexus
Their drivers sipping coffee
Changing channels on the radio
Rehearsing a presentation

All so unheeding
Watch watchwatchwatch
I shake my head in disbelief

Finally the traffic pauses
A clear space
Calm waters
And the old couple
Yes I have begun to feel
A kinship with the ducks
Accomplish the curb
Across from me
Her large orange feet step up
Safe at last I think
But he rests sits
Still on the asphalt
Long enough for me
To worry again
Brief enough for me
To do nothing

Where are they going
This elderly pair
On their morning stroll
There's no pond
No water near
And now
The car shouts behind me
Tells this old man
To get his head
In the game
Our light is green
The people behind
Have places to go
Schedules to meet

5.17-5.18
Mostly drizzle
And heavy rain

Low 60s
Bridgewater International
Poetry Festival
A stranger arrives
And listens
As words fall
Splashing
The auditorium floor
The poets stomp dance slosh
Boots soak
Someone offers an umbrella
Instead
He lifts his face to relentless
   rain
And little rivers phrase
   themselves
Persisting unending
Toward the sea
Clearing winter's debris

5.19
Yesterday
Santa Fe Texas
Another high school shooting
8 students
2 substitute teachers dead
10 wounded
(Heard later 13)
Mid-May Texas Coast weather
Kid wearing black trench coat
He often wears a black trench
   coat
Crazy kids
Who can understand
The weird things they do
Like loving Nazi
And Communist
Iconography
How can you love both

Unless its mere anger
Powerlessness
The frightened roots
That bloom in totalitarianism
Something snapped
Was it because of a girl
Who rebuffed him
Father thinks he was bullied
He was a football player
Who stole
His father's shotgun
And 38
And showed up
For first period
Art class 7:30 am
Shrapnel flies
Tables and art supplies
Splinter and hurl and splash
The kids frightened
In the supply closet
"Surprise!"
The girl face-down
On the floor
One or two blasts
To the head
He shot only those
Whom he didn't like

So
Today
For my presentation
I read 2/14 and 3/34
To polite applause
And handed over
My reading copy
To Taku
From Tanzania
    "Are you a Christian poet?"
Yes sometimes I am

5.23
After so many days
Of storms
Returning
From taking Theo to school
The great shine in my eyes
Once again
The kid in the red helmet
Pedaling the blue bicycle
Up the steep hill
Toward his school
His body strained low
Head over handle bars
Legs shoving shoving

5.29
Sunny today
High 70s/low 80s
A break from a week
Of rain
And another week
Of rain
Predicted
Today Colleen's b/day
Big Five-O
A little gathering this evening
For happy hour
Place called Food Bar Food
So unclever it almost
Rebounds as clever
Colleen likes trendy
Wine weird cocktails
And bowls shaped like
Large broken pecan shells
All angles and juts
Floors walls and ceilings
So hard
Everyone's voices
Ricochet like loosed anxieties

Looking forward to it
Aren't I

Trump world
Has been a deluge
Swirls and eddies
Summit no summit
Maybe summit
With Kim Jong Un
Giuliani and team demeaning
Mueller investigation
Cohen and Russian Taxi guy
Another shooting
In Indiana this time
A good guy coach
Saved the day by tackling
The kid before he shot
Any more
Trade deals with China
To save a company
While getting loans
For Trump and Company
Enterprises and his polling
Just rises and rises
Crazy times and Starbucks is
 closed
Today for training in
 recognizing bias

And rain rain rain
Endicott Maryland main street
 flooding
Second time in two years
Such are our 100-year floods

On a day trip Saturday
Western Maryland
Country road St Mark's Road
Near Middleton
Colleen Theo and I

Wandered upon the remnants
Of Nature's random
And haphazard rage
Just driving toodling along
And then the reverberation
Of near past catastrophe
Sawdust of fallen trees
Swirling in an echo of wind
Something happened here
A storm's clash crashing
In tall branches here still
Not yet silent
Not yet passed fully
Storm ghosts
Environmental aftershocks
The woods ache like
Survivors of car wrecks
Asphalt buckled
Trunks and branches littering
The eroded shoulders
The iron bridge spanning the
 creek
Cluttered with limbs and twigs
Tufts of mud grass
Caught in girders
Piled like broken beaver dams
Fifteen feet above the water

The creek now calm
We paused here
In the memory of roar and
 rumble
And wade in clear water
Theo skips stones
The dance of surface and
 velocity
Resisting weight and gravity
Three four five six skips
Until one stops waits
Or so it seems and sinks

Like a living thing searching
For its one spot
Here I'll sit here's my place
And where did all this fallen
Rain end up
Shooting through here
Like stones thrown down
A hill
Like an avalanche
Of weightless delightful snow
Crushing
Like lava flowing now
In Hawaii
Inching toward the ocean
We are coming through
Where did this rage of water
Stop and settle and rest
Today was our accidental
   witnessing
Sitting beside this gentle
   blessing
Beneath caressing sunlight
The leaves translucent green
Where did that night's
   hopelessness
Cease pounding

June

6.2
Saturday
Rain rain rain
Seems like we are
In flood season
Day moves from shy sun
To skies deluging
Streets flooding
Basements inching
Pools
Water creeping

Much of Friday afternoon
I sat at computer
Completing required training
"Preventing Discrimination
And Sexual Violence
Title IX VAWA and Clery Act
For Faculty and Staff" at EMU

Saturday morning
Drive to Reston
Lake Ann Village Center
Historic District
To read poems
With other members of
Poetry Society of Virginia
At the installation of
Virginia LOVE Statue
With a big rainbow O
Pride LOVE
Got there early
Watched families rent
Paddleboats
Diverse crowd
Hispanic couple and
Two small children
A father with no wedding ring
And two boys
The bigger one in front

With dad paddling
The younger one in back
Seeing where they will have gone
   Stay away
   from the fountain
The teenage dockman warns
(There're some stories behind
That admonition I bet)
Colleen notices two middle-aged
   men
In rainbow tie-dies
One of them in a kilt
Taking photos
In front of Pride LOVE
And offers to take a photo
Of them together
They seem genuinely touched
Thank you yes
They stand together

Luckily no rain this morning
But I drip in humidity
Sweaty love
Wet love
Drenching love
Don't touch me
I'm gross love
Good readings I think
Shouting love lines
So milling people can hear
Just a little bit
Of word or phrase
That might make their steamy
Saturday morning
A little brighter lighter
Commemorative
Farmer's market
   Buy some bread some lettuce
   Some berries farm made
      yogurt

Flowers for home
　　Ah they're talking about
　　　　love
　　Over there
　　Here hold may hand
Could a poem do such a thing
In a public square
In a village
Planned for feelings of leisure
And community
Vision by Robert E. Simon
Early sixties urban planning
For the American middle-class
We do our schtick twice
Stan Galloway Nicole Yurcaba
Susan Notar Sally Toner
Don Carlson with Pat
　　MacIntyre
Her Art Gallery coordinating
Once by the LOVE statue
Once in the farmer's market
Between the soaps
And prepackaged vegan meals
When I finish my two poems
One I wrote when Jorge Flores
Was dying of AIDS
Back when we were learning
What it was that was killing
These beautiful men
And the one I wrote
For William and Kati's
　　wedding
A young woman from the
　　crowd
One that I could see
Was fully listening
Walked over and told me
That she really appreciated
The poem about the wedding
I said thank you

I wrote the poem for my son
She said O you wow
You wrote that
I really liked it
And smiled
I smiled yes I did
Gift given
Gift returned

6.3

When I began yesterday
I thought I would write
About sexual abuse/harassment
It's another storm cloud
In our lives this year
That is always there
But I have not included it
As part of 2018
It's such a large part of
　　2017/18
There I was Friday
Doing my training for EMU
And I need to redo my
　　training
For ACC where I am
Out of compliance
The fact that I am
Out of compliance
When I have been in
　　compliance
Indicates how we believe
We never fully learn
We need to be reminded
And it admits that maybe
Just maybe dare I say it
That the cultural and legal
　　definitions
Of abuse and harassment
Change over time and place
50's What I learned as a child

70s What I learned as a young
   man
90s What I learned as a mature
   adult
10s Is not what I need to know
   now
This does not change the facts
About particular behaviors
This does not justify
Particular behaviors
This just says maybe
And let me say this
Without yelling at me
Is that some of us have not
Always behaved well
But most have been
In compliance
The list has gotten so large
Names piled up
Like cord wood and scraps
And furniture and trash
Rising up for the bonfire
Always Trump Always Trump
Roger Ailes Bill O'Reilly
But now Charlie Rose Mark
Halperin Matt Lauer Tavis
Smiley Alex Jones Mario
Batali Larry Nassar Roy
Moore Al Franken John
Conyers Blake Farenthold
Cristina Garcia Eric
Schniederman James Levine
Kevin Spacey Louis C.K.
Lars von Trier Nelly
Robert "R" Kelly
Stan Lee Sherman Alexie
Junot Diaz Jeffrey Tambor
And the kings
Bill Cosby
Harvey Weinstein

Partial List impartial
Pile it on pile it high
Since April 2017
The number has risen to
220 men almost all men
They are all grabbing pussy
Or cocks or tits or asses

The language so
Repeatable clinical
Sexual legalese predictable

harassment inappropriate behavior sexually charged remarks unwanted touching forcibly kissing misogynistic verbally abusive behavior inappropriate emails inappropriate comments unwanted advances masturbation groping pressing genitals sexual battery child sexual abuse explicit photographs groping hostile working environment exposing unwanted kissing and touching rape sexual assault or battery physically psychologically abusive months-long pattern of sexual harassment groped during photo ops uncomfortable hugs sexist jokes unwanted sexual touching verbally abusive intimidating pressing genitals rape masturbation grinding genitals sexually abusive touched her face without consent controlling coercive video voyeurism sending nude photos of a woman without her knowledge extorting sex from teenage state house page rape exposure masturbation

2018

It would be tedious
If it weren't so horrible
All hope and kindness
Rushing falling tumbling
Into the back hole of human
    disgust
And who exactly
Did we think we were
Strike a match burn baby

And the abused stand around
The pyre and speak back
And the light grows
    Because I am
    A woman
    I can be objectified
    Sexualized reduced
    To a body part
    I was stunned and
    Incredulous I felt demeaned
    I felt put in my place
    He was like an octopus
    His hands were
    Everywhere
    Taking a strong woman
    And tearing her to pieces
    Is his jam
    For the sake
    Of the other women
    And for the sake
    Of my church
    I cannot stay silent
    I tried to walk away
    And he followed me
    Into the kitchen
    Calling me a bitch
    I felt trapped frozen scared
    I was not brave enough
    To say how dare you
    I felt powerless

To say no
He could ruin my career
All of a sudden
There was a hand
On the back of my head
And he shoved his tongue
Down my throat
How do I know
There aren't other victims
How do I know that
He's not still doing this
I still remember his cocky
Grin on his face
Like he got away
With something

Much of Friday afternoon
I sat at computer
Completing required training
"Preventing Discrimination
And Sexual Violence
Title IX VAWA and Clery Act
For Faculty and Staff" at EMU

Much of Sunday afternoon
I sat at computer
Reading this shit
Wondering if I belong
In this list
Wondering if someone
From the dark past
Has something to add
To the chorus of miseries
About me
The wrong me too
The evil me too
The contemptable me too
But I didn't mean
But I was just being
But the times were

But they
But but but but but

Rain rain rain rain
Seems like we are
In flood season
Day moves from sun
To skies deluging
Streets flooding
Basements inching
Pools
Water creeping
And our sins
Are not washed away
If only

6.4
Sunny
A miracle
Mid-70s
Worked all day
On new humanities
On-line class
Starting in July
Based on Barzun's
From Dawn to Decadence
I assume there will be
More on this later
I need to do some exercising

Big thing tonight
Baseball
Valley Baseball League
Young men from colleges
Across the nation
Here in the Shenandoah Valley
Playing ball
June and July
Beautiful cool night

Harrisonburg Turks 4
Winchester Royals 2
Thwack pop of wooden bat
Long arc fly ball
Gasp breath hold
Exhale stand cheer
Triple to deep center
In eighth
Off a slider
Scores two

6.8
Doctor appointment yesterday
Set up back in March
When I had my previous
    appointment
Did I write about that visit
The one I made because
I needed my bp med raised
Cause the bp was rising
Thought I should keep this one
I've been feeling flutters
Like little butterflies
Maybe like moths
Around the lightbulb
In my chest
Nurse EKGed me
Was mum when asked
How it looked
I have my suspicions
I will hear something
Doc says the current med
Makes my pulse too low
A little swelling in the feet
The hydraulic heart
Ain't pumping
Hard enough I guess
Like all the flooding
We've been having in town

All those pumps going
Trying to empty the basements
Chugachugachug
Began new meds today
Chest feels kinda tight
Right now
But just checked bp
And all's fine
I guess
130/82 pulse 59
And I began taking
An anti-depressant
Been feeling blue
Grumpy or haven't you noticed
We can start
A scientific experiment today
Does this long poem
Change its tone

O and we learned
Anthony Bourdain
Killed himself today

6.11
And yet another day
Of rain
Colleen says that normal
For Harrisonburg
By May
Is 14 Inches
By today
We've had 25

Rain falls
Like
Bullets of bad news
You can't run fast enough
Or zig and zag smart enough
To avoid them

There's no umbrella
That can cover you
Big enough or everywhere
You're going to get wet
And then
There are the puddles
Watch out

6.12
I was driving the car
I was in a hurry
In the city
Under elevated train tracks
I was following someone
Or someone was following me
And the road divided
But I was going too fast
Or someone had taken
My lanes
And I needed to slow down
So I put my foot on the brakes
But my foot drops
All the way to the floor
I try again
And search for the place
Where the brakes
Usually engage
It's like massaging
A knot that isn't there
I am thinking why
Don't the brakes work
Again
What's about to happen
I look at the steel beams
Old and rusted
In front of me
And I am thinking
Again
My brakes aren't working

Again
And I am thinking
I know so well
That sensation of unexpected
Absence of resistance
The surprise of empty space
The foot searching
And I am thinking
What did I do all those other times
When my brakes failed me
And then I wake

It's 6:30 the sun is up
I don't have to get out of bed
Because Theo's now
On summer break
But the dream
Has me flustered
It's not that I was about
To have a wreck
It's that
When the brakes failed
When I pushed the foot
All the way to the floor
The sensation felt so normal
So ordinary almost chronic
Like oh this is happening
Again
In the dream
I was not surprised
The person I am
In the dream
Knows this situation well
Even the me
Watching me
In the dream
Thinks
Oh yes
Again

That happening to him
Again
It's only the me
Sitting awake
On the bed
The sun bright
And alive
In the room
Who thinks
This is ridiculous
What's up with this guy
When is he
Ever
Going to fix those brakes

6.13
Wednesday
Lovely Day
No rain
Opened my mouth
At an open mic
In Staunton
At Black Swan Bookstore
And read three poems
From the Old Men book
The other writers
Were welcoming
And I enjoyed their work
Driving home
Slow meandering
Highway 11
At dusk
Countryside and tiny towns
So many stands
Of Orange Day Lilies
So many
They seem like wild natives
Tawny Tiger Ditch Day Lilies
Names for the noble

And the aspirational
Common Invasive
Hemerocallis fulva
Three petals
Three sepals
All opening for a new day
A rise of beauty
The long stalks
Standing tall
These flowers are not shy
They open their throats
And sing rejoiceful
Until the end of evening
No thoughts of tomorrow
Every blossom
Has its day

6.15
Lisa Page
   Trump's never going
   To be President
   Right? Right?!
Peter Strzok
   No. No.
   He won't.
   We will stop it.
Judge Amy Berman Jackson
   The harm
   In this case
   Is harm
   To the administration
   Of justice
   And harm
   To the integrity
   Of the court's system
Donald J. Trump
   So funny
   To watch the fake news
   They are fighting hard
   To downplay the great deal
   With North Korea
   500 days ago
   They would have "begged"
   For this deal—
   Looked like war
   Would break out
   Our Country's biggest enemy
   Is the Fake News
   Promulgated by Fools
Judge Amy Berman Jackson
   This is not middle school
   I can't take his cell phone
   I thought about this long
   And hard
   Mr. Manafort
   I have no appetite
   For this
Donald J. Trump
   I feel badly
   About a lot of it
   Because I think
   A lot of it
   Is very unfair
Judge Amy Berman Jackson
   This hearing
   Is not about politics
   Is not about conduct
   Of the office
   Of the special counsel
Rudolf Giuliani
   Rosenstein
   And Jeff Sessions
   Have a chance
   To redeem themselves
   And that chance comes
   Tomorrow
   It doesn't go beyond
   Tomorrow
   Tomorrow

Mueller should be
    suspended
And honest people
Should be brought in
Impartial people
To investigate these
    people
Like Peter Strzok
Strozk should be
In jail
By the end
Of the week
Donald J. Trump
    Kim Jong Un speaks
    And his people
    Sit up
    At attention
    I want
    My people
    To do
    The same
GOP Chairwoman
    Complacency
    Is our enemy
    Anyone
    That does not embrace
    The @realDonaldTrump
        agenda
    Of making America
    Great again
    Will be making
    A mistake
Rachel Maddow
1995
That is the number
Of kids
The Department of
Homeland Security
Says the US government
Has separated

From their parents
At the southern border
In the six weeks
Between April 19th
And May 31st
That's 46 kids a day
On average

6.19
Tuesday
At my tutoring gig
No appointments at the
    moment
95 degrees today
Woke up early this morning
Feeling clammy
High humidity
Glad I'm inside
Predictions for rain this
    evening
Tomorrow and Thursday
Temps down
To low 80s high 70s
Physical therapy at 8:00am
    today
Third session
Can't tell if we're doing
Much good yet
Adding more and more
    exercises
Nothing I have never done
    before
But I have made none
A regular part
Of my physical life
Iliopsoas
Psoas minor
Hip adductors
Piriformis

Hamstrings
And stretching the back
Engaging the core
That should be the name
Of a book of poems
Engaging the Core

6.21
A two-year old
In red sneakers
Sobs
As her mother
Is searched
Near the banks
Of the great river
They have been traveling
For a month
From Honduras
Escaping gang violence
An unknown risk
Thought lesser
Than the known
A five-year old girl
Cries begs
To call her aunt
The number
A memory
A hope
A lifeline
A toddler
Crawls on a colorful
Alphabet rug
A for Alligator
L for Lion
O for Owl
N for Nutria
E for Elephant
Headless supervisors
In shoes covered

In disposable booties
Hundreds of boys
Fenced caged kenneled
In remodeled box stores/
Stored like overstock
Muraled presidents
Watching silently
The question on everyone's lips
    Where are
    The older girls
And Trump pretends
To undo
What he pretends
He never did
The border guards
Ask the mother
To strip the laces
From her daughter's shoes
Another child weeps
    Papa Papa
    Papa

6.22-6.30
It is really
July 2
5:34 am
I don't know why
I haven't been
Adding to the days
For over a week
Now
I posted the previous poem
On my Facebook page
Don't know why
I did that
Wanted to add
To the conversation
Wanted to record
My dismay

Thought it was
A pretty good
Set of words
Many thumbs up
And sad faces
Over twenty shares
That made me feel
Good
But disappointed
That all those shares
Did not become viral
That's the social media
Ambition
To become an illness
To infect
To require
And inspire
Inoculation
Well
Rachel Maddow
Did not call
From her New York office
Asking to read
The poem
On MSNBC
Oh well
My contagion
Is contained

PT sessions continue
Added exercises
Using a giant ball
Rolling planks
On the floor
Leaning squats
And wabbly presses
Against the wall

Proceeding on creating
New version

Of humanities class
Built on Barzun's big book
I have read the entire thing
800 pages
Grappling with why
He dismisses
And short changes
The twentieth century
So committedly
Sure
He is intellectually
Consistent
All his previous writings
Lead to this moment
But the list of people
And ideals
Is so idiosyncratic
Dada Shaw Dorothy Sayers
No Copeland Thomas Hart
    Benton
Faulkner Steinbeck Ellison
Virginia Woolf James Baldwin
Toni Morrison
Wistawa Szymborska
Frankenthaler Mitchell
Philip Glass John Adams
What was he reading
Looking at listening to
The entire 20th century
How can one
Dismiss it all
As decadent
As demotic

One of my clients
At EMU
From South Korea
A teacher
Wrote about
The Sewol disaster

16 April 2014
Over 300 passengers
And crew
Died
Most of them
High school students
And teachers
Because they obeyed
Orders by ship's officers
To stay below deck
172 disobedients
Survived
Lifted from the sea
By fishers
While National Guard
Dithered
A country drowned
In red tape
And broken processes
Another Johnstown
Another Katrina
Another BP
My client developing
Curricula
To teach independent
Decision making
Individual empowerment
Self-determination

One afternoon
On way to work
At EMU
Rep Goodlatte's
Office porch
And front door
Covered in multi-colored
Posters protesting
His immigration bill
Thought to stop
To photograph

But didn't
Told myself
I would do so
On way home
Then a rainstorm
While at work
And someone
Cleaned up
The soaked voices
Of his constituents
Before I could
Return

   Harley-Davidson
   should never be built
   in another country-never!
   Their employees
   and customers
   are already very angry
   at them.
   If they move,
   watch,
   it will be the beginning
   of the end –
   they surrendered,
   they quit!
   The Aura
   will be gone
   and they will be taxed
   like never before!
   @realDonaldTrump

HOUSE REPUBLICANS
SHOULD PASS
THE STRONG
BUT FAIR
IMMIGRATION BILL,
KNOWN AS
GOODLATTE II,
IN THEIR

AFTERNOON VOTE
TODAY,
EVEN THOUGH THE
    DEMS
WON'T LET IT PASS
IN THE SENATE
PASSAGE WILL SHOW
THAT WE WANT
STRONG BORDERS
& SECURITY
WHILE THE DEMS
WANT OPEN
BORDERS = CRIME
WIN!
@realDonaldTrump

Harley-Davidson
should stay 100%
in America,
with the people
that got you
your success.
I've done so much
for you,
and then this.
Other companies
are coming back
where they belong!
We won't forget,
and neither
will your customers
or your now very HAPPY
competitors!
@realDonaldTrump

Picked up
William and Katie
At Dulles
For a visit
Two nights

In D.C.
Then four more
In Harrisonburg
Haven't seen them
Since wedding
In January
Is there a metaphor
About family
Flying into town
That isn't hackneyed

Silver wings glinting
In bright cerulean skies
Expectation's light
    Light's expectations
    Light's homecoming
    Reunion's sketchbook
    Anticipation
Can't get the line right

What more to say
    I never pushed
    the Republicans
    in the House
    to vote
    for the Immigration Bill,
    either GOODLATTE 1 or 2,
    because it could never
    have gotten
    enough Democrats
    as long as
    there is the 60 vote
    threshold.
    I released
    many
    prior to the vote
    knowing we need
    more Republicans
    to win
    in Nov.

@realDonaldTrump

By moonlight

6.29
Portrait Gallery
MLK
Jefferson
Busboys and Poets
Cornelius Eady
Lincoln Memorial

After dinner
At Busboys and Poets
The four of us
Scavenging books
For dessert
And post-prandial satisfaction
Something strong
And rich
Something sweet
Or warming
I squat on the floor
By the poems
And explore
Cornelius Eady's
Brutal Imagination
Uncle Ben
Jemima
Buckwheat
Susan Smith's
Black fantasy
And the Running Man's
God's sorry
Sense of humor

Final destination
For the day
Before heading back
To the hotel
The Lincoln Memorial

6.30
Protest Lafayette Park

I don't know
What is wrong
With me
These two days
Here in D.C.
With Colleen
With my son
And his wife
Introducing them
The city
That is the center
Of our life
Political/historical
This is the theme
Of this book
But I am
Overwhelmed
Too much
Too much

    My people
    Were Refugees
    Too
    Just for all
    Families belong
    Together
    This is some
    Nazi Shit
    All in All
    You are just
    Another brick
    In the wall
    I can't believe
    I still

Have to protest
This shit

July

7.4
Independence Day
Warm again
After living in Texas
For fifty-plus years
Can't call it hot
Noon
High eighties
Humidity steams
With Will and Katie
And Colleen
And a couple
Hundred neighbors
Under the shade
Of the courthouse oaks
We listen
To the Sons
Of the American Revolution
Read The Declaration
Of Independence
A man in a dark suit
And a red tie
At a podium
Atop the courthouse
Eastern steps
Wiping his brow
With a folded handkerchief
Projecting his voice
Authority and honor
And seven scruffy
Fellow citizens
Dressed in mock
Revolutionary soldier garb
Bearing arms
Lined up beneath him
At the foot of the steps
Looking like extras
On minimum pay
Glad not to have
Any speaking lines

If I were British
I would be ashamed
These no counts
Defeated me
Somebody in the crowd
Has a flag
With thirteen stars
In a circle
Others have tiny flags
On sticks
Some brought lawn chairs
Some sit on blankets
Some stand erect
T-shirts and button downs
Cargo shorts jeans
And summer chinos
In coral and green
Some children and dogs
Run free unaware
Of the long loose leash
Of history
    When in the course
    Of human events
And
    We hold these truth
And
    Life liberty
And
    The pursuit of happiness
Whatever that means
Big words
In capital letters
Tossed around
Rights People Creator
Despotism Tyranny
Laws Representation
Laws of Naturalization
Administration of Justice
Standing Armies
Civil Power

Cruelty Perfidy
Free and Independent
Our Lives our Fortunes
Our honor
We applaud
We believe
We are happy
The English teacher in me
Thinks it's a dandy argument
If this…. then that
Who could disagree
And
The seven guns explode
Smoke drifts and thins
Over the dispersing crowd

As we round
The one-way streets
That circle
The courthouse
History keeps moving
On the southwest corner
Three homeless men
Cool in the shade
Of the pagoda
Marking the old spring
Where Brother John Kline
Imprisoned
For his peaceful ways
During the Civil War
Wrote the chorus
To "The Prisoner's Song"
    We'll go home
    As soon as freed
    A holy life
    With God to lead
    Yes we'll go home
    And to spend our days
    In peace
    Till life shall end

There are many ways
To embody
Independence

7.5
Returned my son
And his wife
To Dulles
For their flight home

Before that
A detour
For Skyline Drive
Fluttering ribbon
Of a road
And ever present
Promise of hope
Across the next valley

A stop at distillery
Near Sperryville
G&Ts
Beneath dappled shade
Along a whispering creek
The silence
Of a long goodbye

7.6
Depression is
The glooming
In the garden
With no wind

Today
I told Colleen
About the anti-depressant
I was taking
And my decision

To stop
Taking it
It made me
Dull inside
A still pond
The stones
Fall in
But no splash
No waves

7.10
I barbecued chicken breasts
Colleen steamed green beans
And sliced large red tomato
From the farmer's market
Last minute decision
To go to movies
Will You Be My Neighbor
Love
Love your neighbor
Love yourself
You are special
You are my beloved child
You are a lamb of god
When the movie ends
The audience
This Sunday night
A mere eight couples
Strayed throughout
The theater
Remain seated
In the rising light
Silent
Unable to disconnect
The theater
A church
A home for hope
A home for shame
And regret

No one wanted
To leave
To return
To the world
We have built
Entertaining our selves
With cynical
Shameless
Rude
Cruel
Excitements

Home
Parking the car
Behind our home
We stand in cool grass
And watch
Sighing
Dozens of fireflies
In the dusk
Here
Here
There
Here
Brief lights
But more lights
Always no matter what
More lights

7.12-7.13
Travel day
Bus to Union Station
DC
Amtrak from Union Station
DC
To Union Station
Chicago
What's up with this
Union Stations

Uniting everywhere
I need to look
That up
Otherwise
I am getting nowhere
(And it's no Utopia)
Crowded cars
With a group of students
Returning from class trip
To the nation's capital
Can't be sorry about that
At the tables
In the observation car
They laugh and joke
Filling out worksheets
A couple of these girls
Large breasted
Are dressed
In the least
Amount of cloth
Possible
Canyons of cleavage
And double untanned
    crescents
Below the cloud
Of tiny gym shorts
Thought of taking photo
To send to Colleen
Saying I am so glad
I am not the father
Of girls
Thought better of whipping
Out my iPhone
As like Italo Calvino's
Palomar
I realize
That I too am being watched
And possibly
Misjudged

Bad night sleeping
Corridor light
Mooning
Above me in aisle seat
Ended up
On floor
In observation car
For a couple
Of dark night
Of the soul hours
Of shifting sleep
Back to assigned seat
Tied my bandana
Around my eyes
Like I was
Standing
Against the wall
Ready for execution
Just relax
Lyman
Do you have
Any last words

I'm innocent?
I was only seeing
What was in front of me?
It was coffee and light
That kept me up
Not guilt?
Not yet?

We will be
Two and half hours
Late
Pulling into
Union Station

I listen to Ry Cooder
    "You should
        Have told me

You was married
Baby"

7.14
I have been
Shielding myself
From Trump
Lately

Such daily disasters
Who can keep up
What does it
Do to you me
To keep up
Or not to keep up

Blowing his way
Around Europe
Turning scowls
Into handshakes
And smiles
Into fists

I am going
To read in
Hannah Arendt's
The Life of the Mind
For a few days
While I am
In the mountains
I'm curious
What she means
By Will
Maybe I should be
Reading *Origins of
  Totalitarianism*
Or *Eichmann in Jerusalem*
  "The banality of evil"

Read a Facebook post
By a friend
George Randall Leak III
  Earlier had a long
  chance conversation
with a neighbor
I've never met,
a young white man
in his 20s
who declared himself
a Trump supporter
who chimed in
on a conversation
I was having with Robin.

I listened
to this young man
for some time
and argued with him
about
how separating families
of asylum seekers
was not only a violation
of the Golden Rule
but a politically
inept move
not to mention
an immoral one.
He openly declared
himself a Racist
and said
he not only thought
Black Lives Matter
was a stupid movement
funded entirely by George
  Soros
& other Globalists
but the Civil Rights
  Movement
was a mistake

and, in fact
ending Slavery
was the biggest mistake
in the history
of the United States
because Slavery
was an "act of generosity"
on behalf
of Americans.

I doubt
I convinced him,
but I certainly
gave him plenty
of gristle to chew on.

Where I really gave him
food for thought
was talking
about the benefits
of the New Deal
and how they led
to an unprecedented
sustained period
of economic growth
to put it simply
because of the ricochet
    effect
of raising all boats.
And ever since
we abandoned
many of these policies
we've been in a period
of economic stagnation,
that's not only bad for us
regular people,
but for the rich.
His friends
Wondered at how
He had the patience

To talk to this young man
For such a long time

From the train from Chicago
To Las Vegas New Mexico
In the middle of Western
    Kansas
Eastern Colorado
I watch the wasted landscape
Brown grass and sand
Sliced ravines
Eroded gullies
Sagging barbed wire
A random short starved
Juniper shrub
Nothing taller than head high
A random short starved
Steer
In towns
Piles of scrap wood
Tangled broken metal
Tractored concrete shards
Auto carcasses
Scattered appliances
(Shitted not sung)
Un-painted/wind-scoured
Buildings
With cracked
Or missing windows
Symbols of doomed inability
To husband past prosperity
Always the lost ounces
Of hope
Rusting rotting
I think someone needs
To tear down
Haul away
The accusations
At one stop
Two old unshaven white men

Limp the suitcases
Toward the station
Freshly painted
And proclaimed
Reclaimed
By DC money
I thought
The problem is
That the young have left
The small mid-sized towns
No one is left
With the strength
To do the heavy work
Of removing
The obsolescent debris
Of post war fortune

7.15-7.20
Most days
Middle 80s
Brief afternoon rains
8,100 feet
Outer spills
Of the Sangre de Cristos
New Mexico
With fifteen men
Mostly longtime friends
From Austin
Whom I have missed
Like family
Since moving to Virginia
In September
Wounded hearts healed
The tailend
I guess
Of the much maligned
Men's movement
Of the late eighties/
Early nineties

Ok dear sophisticated reader
Make fun if you wish
Men crying because
Their fathers were assholes
Their mothers were cunts
(I am quoting, of course)
Shaking with the memories
Of being beaten with belts
Shamed repeatedly
For making the mistakes
That help one mature
A man in grief divorcing
Wife of thirty years
Because she decided
She just didn't want
To keep growing
(No blame
Her choice
He still loves her
But he shrivels inside)
An artist frustrated
Because the praise
And awards
Don't pay the property tax
A gay man
(Do I really have to
Enumerate his oppressions
And sorrows)
A dedicated grandfather
Saying goodbye
To the daughter
Who died of opioid overdose
Make fun
If you wish
But I see saints
Redeeming our world
Cleansing the toxins
Of our poisoning lives
Good men
No more wounded

Than you
But more intolerant
Of forces of hate
And greed and fear
And shame
Yes that means you
That "clever" remark
You made about
What a co-worker
Wore to work today
The "relaxing" hours you spent
On the X-box shooting
Somebody/anybody
Allbodies
The "tolerance"
You proudly sighed
At the checkout line
When that woman's
Child threw a fit
Demanding candy
Productively placed
To tempt the tired
And anxious
The pride you shine
Because you
Can hide your wounds
And win
This game of life
Sullen and superior

Enough
Sorry for the rant
I wish you well

So five days
On a mountain
With men
Deliberately
And consciously
Performing

Soul/body
Surgery

What ails
You
Let's talk about
It
Let's express it
Ex-press it
From the body
And replace
The harmful
With the healthful

Still making fun
That's your symptom
What ails you
Begin there

Our mornings
In cool silence
Mindful walks
In shivering Aspens
Qi Gong
With Ponderosa Pines
Gather the sun
Sweep the floor
Shoot the arrow
Clutch the tiger
Release the poison
Replenish the nutrients
Receive the vision
Claim the future

Days in a circle
Nights in prayer

    There is nothing
    Truly wrong
    With any of us

Before with me
It has always been
Enlarge
Always
Both/and
This time
I will leave
Something behind

I always choose
To stand
In God's
Peripheral vision

I am a man of ashes
And dust
And broken bark
And fallen leaves

I watch birds
At the feeder
While men share
Their secret horrors

When/where
Did I begin
To think
That I was
Inadequate
That I was not unique
Irreplaceable
And necessary
In Mystery's plan

The morning winks
Wink back

The rich coarse green
Of the forest
Across the valley

In the afternoon sun
Why not act
Like a man
Who has faith

I am
Nowhere
Near
Civilization
And
I am
Full

    Eating the bread
    Of this world
    And doing the work
    Of that world
        —prayer from Andy

I am human
And nothing human
Is alien to me
    —Terence

I love
What comes
And
I love
What goes
I love
What comes
And
I love
What goes
I love
What comes
And
I love
What goes
I love

What comes
And
I love
What goes

From reading
Hannah Arendt
Willing
  Say no to my now
  And thus
  Create my own future

What we do
On the mountain
Is to empty
The present
Of the past
So that
We can
Will the future
Into being

Yes
In a moment of joy
I wrapped by arms
Half-way around
An old Ponderosa Pine
Allowed its spice
To infuse me
It ascended fifty/sixty feet
Almost all the way up
Its once long
Strong green branches
Are broken stubs
Nubs and dead limbs
That which before
Had balanced and sustained it
Unneeded
And falling away
Yet its crown

Rises into the sunlight
Arms reaching
In revelatory glee
Glowing
Glorious green
Growing

7.20-7.21
In a motel
I avoid the news
And watch
Highlights
Of the Tour de France
Go round and round

7.22
Oh
what I missed
  I have great confidence
  In my intelligence
  People
  They said
  They think it's Russia
  I have President Putin
  He just said
  It's not Russia.
  I don't see
  Any reason
  Why it would be
And then
  In a key sentence
  In my remarks
  I said the word
  Would
  Instead of
  wouldn't
  The sentence
  Should have been:

'I don't see any reason
why I wouldn't,
or why it wouldn't
be Russia,'

Sort of a double negative.

So you can put that in,
And I think
That probably
Clarifies things
Pretty good
By itself

I wouldn't
Have
Great confidence
In his intelligence
People

    There was
    No
    Colution *[sic]*

7.24
Li Po tells me
I should be
Drinking
That's a happy thought
Maybe I should
Flee the house
Maybe I should
Take a walk
Beyond the milk spills
Of city lights
Maybe I should
Listen to the moon
Sing to me
Of broken urns

Dipped into cool rivers
And lifted out
Dripping
Already half empty
Maybe I should
Stumble
Into a stranger's yard
Fall on my back
Let hours of dew
Soak me through
And through
And simply listen
Listen to the voices
Of someone else's house

7.28
Beautiful mild
Summer day
Low eighties
Sunny
Three or four days
Late writing/posting
Review/test 2
For online humanities class
Summation/Distillation
Of what I think
Is most important
The take away
My version of Hirsh's
Cultural literacy
I guess
What we are exposed to
What we study
What we remember
A funnel
But we are more
Than leaky containers
Being filled
Who knows what

Remains inside
And for how long
We are also sponges
Stuff gets absorbed
We become soggy
With knowledge
Until we are squeezed
To make room
For more
But some old wetness
    remains
Anyway
I had a good time
Today
At Starbucks
With Colleen
Re-minding myself
Of the highlight reel
Of The Enlightenment
    The life of man,
    solitary, poor, nasty,
    brutish, and short
But
    no one ought to harm
    another in his life,
    health, liberty,
    or possessions:
    for men being
    all the workmanship
    of one omnipotent,
    and infinitely wise maker
But then
    Man is born free;
    and everywhere
    he is in chains.
    One thinks himself
    the master of others,
    and still remains
    a greater slave
    than they.
And must be reminded
    the most perfect education,
    in my opinion,
    is such an exercise
    of the understanding
    as is best calculated
    to strengthen the body
    and form the heart.
    Or, in other words,
    to enable the individual
    to attain such habits of
        virtue
    as will render it
        independent.
    In fact, it is a farce
    to call any being virtuous
    whose virtues do not result
    from the exercise
    of its own reason.
    This was Rousseau's opinion
    respecting men.
    I extend it to women,
All the while
People assert
    It is the best
    Of all possible worlds
But eventually
We must be reminded
    To tend our own gardens
For although
    man's first disobedience,
    and the fruit
    Of that forbidden tree,
    whose mortal taste
    Brought death into the
        world,
    and all our woe,
    With loss of Eden,
    till one greater man
    Restore us, and regain

  the blissful seat,
Maybe we should remember
That making sense
Of our little individual
Lives and the lives
Of our fellow citizens
And our fellow humans
That we should
  Know, then, thyself,
  presume not God to scan;
  The proper study
  of mankind
  is man.
  Placed on this isthmus
  of a middle state,
  A being darkly wise,
  and rudely great:
  With too much knowledge
  for the sceptic side,
  With too much weakness
  for the stoic's pride,
  He hangs between
But most of us will
Prance and dance
With Lully and Moliere
Keeping the future waiting
Our selves being
Caught and reduced
In current fashions
Of Spanx and skinny jeans
  Which I thought
  I should never
  Be able to get on

(As Truman might accuse)
And our terrier
Climbs the narrow
Stairs to curl
At my feet
While early
Nightfall pounds
Our copper roof
I think
He is scared
But maybe
He believes
That if the maw
Of thunder
Should assault
He must
Be near
To snarl
And nip
At danger's ankles
While I shout
And swing
A lighted branch
At the wild claws
Of all things
Dark and nameless

7.30
These crazy summer
Afternoon storms
I work upstairs
Reading or typing

August

8.6
Sunny
Mid-80's
Been like this
For a while
Except for interruptions
Of rain
We are about 8 inches
Above normal
For the year
Past couple months
Have been very soggy
Discovered yesterday
On drive with my sisters
Who visited for two days
Trees uprooted
By hurricane type winds
Trunks lying on the ground
Like dead bodies
Root balls ripped up
And exposed
Like bare asses
You feel guilty looking
At their revealed vulnerability
For fifty minutes
On August 1
The winds rushed through
And trees
Randomly
Let go
Gave up
Fell over
Two here
One there
Another down
The road
So close to the house
A couple more
In the field
Dozens over all

A massacre
I have been so busy lately
With keeping my
Humanities class rolling
Grading essays
Posting comments
And readings
Something from *Mein Kampf*
Something from Hannah
Arendt
Auden's Unknown Citizen
Ginsberg's *Howl*
As we begin closing
Summer semester
Aiding my grad students
At EMU
I hadn't kept up with news
Of course
Always the rage about Trump
But what is happening
Right around me
Winds and rain
It is all
So much
Wind and rain
Ripping us up
And tossing us
Drenching us

I don't know
If poetry
In short lines
Is an art
For flooding seasons
The eye roves
Rushed
Receiving
But not seeing
I need to slow
Things down

Take the time
To see
With the second
Inward
Eye

8.10
Driving to Chapel Hill
To see sisters again
This time
To celebrate Diane's
Seventy-fourth
We stop at Blacksburg
For the night
Virginia Tech
It is one of the things
We do
Visit college campuses
Who knows
Maybe there is a job
There for Colleen
Someday
Maybe the boys
Theo this time
Will remember
That college
Is their future
The meadow
Of their imagination
Like a campus
Filled with possibility

And of course
We also kneel
At memorial sites

16 April 2007

This half fairy ring

Of stones
Of stumps
Twenty-seven students
Five teachers
Their arc
Part of the widening arc
Of bodies
Nation-wide
The spreading rhizome
Of murder's perennial
Blooming
Dolomite limestone
Blocks buried
Feet first
So that head
Stones
Speaking their names
Face you
Accuse you
Ask you
What have you done
Besides weep
You stand
In a necrotic daze
The hands of angels
Reach around you
What do they garden
Into the hole
In your chest

Later in afternoon
Colleen's second college
For the day
Guilford
Across the street
I see a sign
Directing us
Away from
The main entrance
Toward Randall Jarrell's grave

Lyman Grant

But time is short
And graveyards large
Theo and I drive
Around the edges
Peeking in
While Colleen walks the dog
No one sees
Jarrell's chiseled name
Sunk into prone stone
Like a book
Dropped carelessly
Among the unmown grass
Today
Driving on
Toward Chapel Hill
I muse
O to be a student
With my stack
Of dreams
And this god
Buried
Across that
Busy road

8.11
A morning
At the Belted Goat Coffee
Shop
In Fearrington Village
With my brother-in-law
De-Café Au Lait
And free internet
Grading the final essays
Of the humanities class
While he unearths secrets
From his ancestral notes
And at McIntyre's Books
Reading poems
By Neruda and Transtromer

Excuse me
But it is a sign
Of unearned privilege
To relax into cushioned calm
Allowing words to pinch
The skin of consciousness
To welcome the vulnerability
Of acute perception
To speak quietly intimately
Into a silence
Because you know
You will be heard

The evening
At my sister Barbara's home
The generations ring
The kitchen island
To sing
To my sister Diane's health
Continuing
Her favorite cake
Flaked coconut icing
Alit with the legacy
Of parenting's
Awakenings

8.14
Hello
My name is Lyman
I am a chip-oholic
I am addicted
To crunch
To chomp
To munch
To grind
To the salt
Of life
To Pretzels
To Bugles

To Tostitos
To Funyuns
To the high
Blood pressure
Of life
To the tire
Around my waist
To the dull dead
Release
From the tedious
Stupidities
Of life
In the 21st
Century
To the bite
Mastication
The chew
Of refined
Banalities
Ground
Mushed
Reconstituted
Shaped and reformed
Baked and fried
All of which
Is to say
That I awarded myself
Today my 30-day
No-chip chip
Hooray

8.12-8.17
A Dialogue between Spirit and
   Flesh

Spirit
   What responsible
   & right-thinking adult
   can point
   to you
   as a role model
   for our youth?
   Whenever you spew
   Your lies, insults,
   and polarizing
   hate speech
   against fellow Americans,
   I think of its harmful impact
   on our young people
   and the way they talk,
   act, & treat
   others.
Flesh
   While I know
   it's 'not presidential'
   to take on a low life
   and while I would rather
   not be doing so
   I know
   the Fake News Media
   will be working overtime
   to make even Wacky Omarosa
   look legitimate
   as possible. Sorry!
Spirit
   You're absolutely right.
   If you were 'presidential,'
   you would focus
   on healing the rifts
   within our Nation
   being truthful
   about the challenges
   we face, & showing the world
   that America is still
   that shining beacon
   of freedom, liberty,
   prosperity, & goodness
   that welcomes all.
Flesh

When you give
a crazed, crying lowlife
a break,
and give her a job
at the White House,
I guess
it just didn't work out.
Good work
by General Kelly
for quickly firing
that dog!
Spirit
It's astounding
how often you fail
to live up
to minimum standards
of decency, civility, &
   probity.
Seems like you
will never understand
what it means
to be president,
nor what it takes
to be a good, decent,
& honest person.
So disheartening,
so dangerous
for our Nation.
Flesh
As your president
I have decided to revoke
your security clearance
You have recently
leveraged your status
as a former high-ranking
official with access
to highly sensitive
information
to make a series
of unfounded
and outrageous allegations
– wild outbursts
on the internet
and television –
Your lying
and recent conduct,
characterized
by increasingly
frenzied commentary,
is wholly inconsistent
with access
to the Nation's
most closely held secrets
and facilitates
the very aim
of our adversaries,
which is to sow
division and chaos.
Spirit
This action
is part of a broader effort
to suppress freedom of speech
& punish critics.
It should gravely worry
all Americans,
including intelligence
professionals,
about the cost
of speaking out.
My principles
are worth far more
than clearances.
I will not relent.
An Angel
You have revoked
one of the finest
public servants
I have ever known,
a man
of unparalleled integrity,

whose honesty and
    character
have never been in question,
except by those
who don't know him.
I would consider
it an honor
if you would revoke
my security clearance
as well,
so I can add my name
to the list of men
and women
who have spoken up
against your presidency.
Through your actions,
you have embarrassed us
in the eyes
of our children,
humiliated us
on the world stage
and, worst of all,
divided us as a nation.
Our criticism
will continue
until you become
the leader
we prayed
you would be.
  A Choir of Angels
    All of us believe
    it is critical
    to protect
    classified information
    from unauthorized
       disclosure.
    But we believe
    equally strongly
    that former government
       officials

have the right
to express
their unclassified views
on what they see
as critical
national security issues
without fear
of being punished
for doing so.
The country
will be weakened
if there is
a political litmus test
applied before
seasoned experts
are allowed
to share their views.

And where is Gina Haspell?

8.19
I kept waiting
For the moment
When that voice
That sometimes hides
Inside
Would be shaken
Awake
Like my teenage son
In the early morning
When he has forgotten
That today is a school day
That shock jolt
The body jumping
The mind beginning
To sprout itself
Out of its darkness
Unaware
As if one's hands
Were outstretched

Poking massaging
The nothingness
Expectant of what
Moving by faith
Encased
Slowly edging
Toward recollection
Not so marvelously
Emerging into light
But just imperceptively
Unblackening
The unknown
Redacted knowledge
That everything
Was once okay
And will be again
And that I am lucky
That today is that day

8.22
You know
You are having
A bad week
When your wife
Pleads guilty
With the nation's youth
Not to cultivate
Your pugilistic habits
When your definition
Of friendship
Is someone
Who doesn't *rat*
When you scuttle
To West Virginia
To sing the oxymoronic
Elegy of *clean coal*
With your favorite hillbilly
    choir
When one good guy
Heroes your regard

Going down
On eight counts
And another (former) good
    guy
Stands in the ring
Taking punches
As you go down
With him
    If anyone
    Is looking for
    A good lawyer
    I would strongly suggest
    That you don't retain
    The services
    Of Michael Cohen
    @realDonaldTrump

8.25
As should be obvious
To everyone
By now
Past and present
Present and past
Are aswirled
Today I returned
To a couple
Of July days
And membered them
Into the body
Of this poem
By remembering them
Embodying
The mists of memory
Into the residue
Of words

Does it matter
That the matterer
Always knew

That the matter
Would be mattered
When time allowed
And when the matter
Insisted it mattered

The sculptor's
Dilemma
Where in time
Does a memory
Be
Long

Do memories long
For a future
Or
To be
Re-placed
Into the past

In any case
This is not
The only thing
I wrote today

Did you know
That when you
Read the fourth
And fifth of July
That you were
Really reading
The twenty-fourth
Of August
Did/does/will
It matter

8.27

There are many reasons
Not to go to war
When others do
But one of them
Is not that
Your daddy is rich
Or that have bone spurs
In your pampered feet

There are many reasons
Not to honor those
Who go to war
When others do
But one of them
Is not that you
Are rich
And like to play golf
And build resorts
For other rich heels
That your chaotic soul
Could never toe the line
Of military discipline

There are many reasons
Not to honor the dead
When almost everybody
Else in the nation does
But one of them
Is not that you
Avoided the draft
Never trained for war
Never was captured
Never was tortured
Never returned home
A hero
Never ever served
Your country
Because your sole desire
Is to get richer
And richer
Through bankruptcies
Cheating on taxes

Robbing workers
Of their pay
And collaborating
With corrupt oligarchs
From the worst places
In the world

There are many reasons
Not to admire
Our president
When others still do
And one of them
Is that today
He refused to fly
The American flag
Above the White House
At half-mast
To honor
John McCain
Until his body is buried
In the hallowed ground
Of the Naval Academy
Where Trump delicate
Blistered callused
And ingrown
Dare not step
With his cowardly
Bullish boorish
Tender tender feet

8.30
Imagine this
A window high
On the wall
So that it opens
Only to sky

And imagine
A mirror high
On the opposite wall
So that it sees
Only the window
Opening
To clouds and sky

And imagine
A justice
That is not
About punishing
Taking away
A hand or ear
An eye a friend
A child
But imagines
Restoring
What has been
Lost
Revealing
Something boundless
And returns
To the victim
The one
Missing thing
A watch these hands
A kiss that smile
On the face
Of a lover
When the day
Begins

Imagine returning
Home from work
Listening to the dreams
Of the young
And being so full
Of the language
Of hope
That when I sit
In my room

Reading Szymborska
Like this evening
And the sky opens
And cleanses
The exhausted air
Both inside and out
Something in me
Flashes
And shakes
And thunders back
Like a memory
Like an echo
Like a storm
Like its calm

September

9.8
Oh my god
It's been nine days
Since I opened
This document
And added any words
I can't let that happen
A large bit of my ego
Is attached
To continuing this thing
You know
I want to be able
To say
"I did this
I thought about
Writing a big poem
About 2018
I committed to it
I began it
On January 1
I continued it
And eventually
On December 31
I completed it"
It does no good
Really
To say
"I committed to
Twelve months
And made it
For eight"
This cannot be
A work in progress
For years and years
Not like
An unfinished draft
Of a novel
That I could pick
Up again
When things get

Less busy
A couple of years
Later
And say oh
Where was I
Oh yes
John McCain just died
I'll pick up the story there
If this crazy project
Has anything going for it
It is its immediacy
It is its fly by the pants
Build it as you go
Unplanned oops stop the
   presses
I have to go take a pee
Living it day-by-day
Reporting of the moment
It is not memory
It is not construction
It is supposed to be
Merely and only presence
And I have not been
Present here

Not that you would feel that
You are not reading this book
I wouldn't think
Day-by-day
Like a quote
For every morning
Flip calendar
Wow that would be
Something very weird
I would think
To stretch this sucker
Out for the year
Whew
Not recommended
Though it's a bit late

To not recommend that

So where have I been
First
Classes started again
Last week
But the first week
Of classes
Is mostly
Here is the syllabus
And you tell me
Who you are
I'll tell you who I am
Getting to know
Each other
Kind of activities
Sound of Music
Kind of activities
This week second week
Preparation
Assignments
Grading
Getting up early
Always thinking
Two days ahead
I have said
Haven't I
That I have begun
My third part time job
I like saying that
It lets me feel
Like a martyr
To the family
Aren't I a good
Husband and father
We will have the money
So
Jacob can go to Costa Rica
For a Jan term class
So
Theo can go to Chicago
For a school trip
So
Colleen can do a conference
Or two
(Also so
I can go to Asheville for a
    conference
On Black Mountain College
And Austin for a reading
And see William
But I don't want to admit that
Publicly
Doesn't do much
For my martyr status)
In addition
To my two online classes
I am still tutoring
18 hours a week
And now I have added
Two more composition classes
At EMU
This is more
Than full-time work
And I am supposed
To be retired
Poor poor pitiful me
Violins please

Why am I telling you this
Why do I feel
That I have to justify
Myself to you

Anyway
I have been busy
Really

And then
Colleen and I

Have been wasting
Our evenings
Binge watching
As it is now called
What an awful
Shameless/shamefilled
Culture we live in
Everything is binging
Massive plates of food
Big gulps
Beer poured through funnels
Extreme sports
So few things
In moderation
Even watching television
(Even a poem
We might mention)
Colleen and I
Have been binging
On a television program
Now on Netflix
Scandal
Yes I am ashamed
It is a minor
Personal scandal
Over the past
Couple of weeks
That I have sacrificed
Fifty/sixty hours
Of my life
Hours I will never recover
Watching this show
Lord forgive me
For what I have done
For what I have left undone
I have not loved you
With my whole heart

But I think
What really stopped/stumped

me
Was John McCain's funeral
I didn't mean to watch it
There for awhile
Back in 90s
He seemed like
A pretty interesting guy
Maverick and all that
Good with the press
And all that
Karl Rove screwed him
In South Carolina
(McCain has a black baby
 —so are we surprised
  At Trumpsters' racism
  The Republicans
  Courted racism
  For decades)
But he was gun(g)-ho
To invade Iraq
He welcomed Sarah Palin
To the lower 48
He supported Trump's tax
Reductions for the rich
Started out ok
I guess
But this century
He became more
And more conservative
Sold out? Political necessary?
Does it matter?
My point?
There are many reasons
Not to mourn
The death of John McCain
Other than the fact
That we mourn the death
Of anyone
And anyone
Who has demonstrated

2018

Bravery and fortitude
As he did in Hanoi

But he won
many friends
voting that once
against McConnell's
and Trump's
attempts to kill
the ACA

So I didn't mean
To tune in
To the funeral
But I did
I like listening
To Chris Matthews
And Jon Meacham
Then one thing
Led to another
And three hours
My life
Were gone
Into another collage
Of sound
Medley of eloquence
Kaleidoscope
Of portentousness
Cornucopia
Of conspicuous corn
    "Today is only one day…"
  We gather to mourn
  The passing
  Of American greatness
  The real thing
  Not cheap rhetoric
  From men who will
  Never come near
  The sacrifice
  Those that live lives

Of comfort and privilege
While he suffered
And served
Honor intangible
Not obligatory
No code
Inward compulsion
Free of self interest
Not personal ambition
Society lives beyond
Necessities of the moment
Love honor nobility

A way of life
A code
A set of public virtues
Strength and purpose
To life to country
Not defined by borders
But founding values
Freedom human rights
Opportunity democracy
Equal justice under law
    "Today is only one day
    In all the days…"
Most people feel
A longing
For what is lost
And cannot be restored
The happy casual beauty
Of youth
Something better
Can endure and endure
Our last moment
When we sacrifice
For something greater
Than ourselves
Being unpredictable
A little contrarian
No interest conforming

To prepackaged
What should be
   "No one of us
   If they have character
   Leaves behind
   A wasted life"
Commit to something
Bigger than yourself
Dignity does not stop
At borders
And cannot be erased
By dictators
The America
Of John McCain
Has no need
To be made great again
He loved freedom
With a passion
Who knew its absence
John didn't have
Patience one virtue
He did have
Forgiveness a great virtue
America
Was always great
   "Today is only one day
   In all the days
   That will ever be…"
Celebrate
Striving to be better
To do better
To be worthy
Of the great inheritance
Our politics
Our public life
Our public discourse
Can seem small
And mean and petty
Bombast and insult
Phony controversies

Manufactured outrage
Politics pretends
To be brave tough
But is born of fear
John called on us
To be bigger
To be better
Our country
Not a physical place
But a carrier
Of enduring
Human aspirations
Advocate for oppressed
Defender of peace
Promise unwavering
Undimmed unequalled
Democracy renewed
Reaffirming principles
On which it was founded
America
Somehow always
Found leaders
Up to that task
At the time of greatest need
   "Today is only one day
   In all the days
   That will ever be
   But what will happen
   In all the other days
   That ever come
   Can depend
   On what you do today"
And my father
Would have said
"Sure it's corn
But it's good corn."

The whole time
Looking at the great
And near great

The famous
And near famous
In America's cathedral
Pale Episcopalians
Hymns and readings
Danny Boy
I wondered
Am I witnessing
The counter revolution
The return of the oligarchy
The Roman Republic
Reasserting itself
Against mad Caesar
Who in that congregation
Was sharpening their knives
Or was this
The last gathering
The funeral
Of the old guard
The final goodbye
The lilies dropped
Into the grave
Plunk plunk
The clods of clay
Fall knocking
Clunk clunk
On the closed casket
Of the body politic
The admission
That our old nobility
Has become sad
Whispers of dusty words
Dry lips gray hair
And black suits
Worn thin
In the ass

9.9
Sunday morning

Heavy rain
Overnight
Overcast
And 56 degrees
Through open windows
I hear cars slish
By on slick streets
Then silence
Then Colleen downstairs
Calling to the dog
The high hum
Of a truck far away
About to shift gears
A car approaching
From the other direction
A bird or frog whirling
Behind
Stereo Surround Sound
And inside
If I listen
Tinning of my old ears

    Thank you
    To Chairman Kim
    We will both prove
    everyone wrong
    There is nothing
    like good dialogue
    from two people
    that like each other
    Much better
    than before
    I took office
    @realDonaldTrump

What is going on?

9.12
I think

I have made
A big mistake
Saying that I would
Teach these two
Freshman composition classes
I am starting to pick on them
The wounds of their
    indifference
The scabs that seal their
    ignorance
I don't think I like them
I don't think they like me
I want to scrub them
To raw them a bit
And maybe
That is not healthy
I was once
A popular teacher
A funny teacher
Maybe an effective teacher
Now they bore me
Maybe I bore me
But I don't want
To entertain them
I think they want me
To make writing fun
Writing can be fun
But that's an inside job
I ask a girl
To create a thesis
Topic and comment
For essay 1
About a place
They feel or don't feel
At home in
    "My house is small"
I ask her to add
A comparison
A simile
"My house is a small as…."

"I don't know…
    Whatever…."
And she puts
Head on the table
I feel my words
Go in her
But they do not
Even echo in there
They just fall and fall
And fall
I don't want to play
Either
I think I have grown
Tired of artifice
And decoration
Of pizzazz
    "Make your class
    Like a Ted-Talk"
    The official advice
    From beyond
I am becoming
A Rothko painting
An Albers
A Diebenkorn
Just shape and color
No representation
No definition
No subject
Other than what you see
I am tired
Of pretending
But I should remember
The class is at 8am
Three mornings a week
No one wants to be there
This early
And everyone is 18
I should remember
Wayne Booth's essay
"Boring from Within"

About the problem
With the Freshman essay
That no one can change
Freshmen write them
Maybe I am bitter
Maybe I have made
A big mistake
Maybe I should go
To my next class
And see
If I can talk
With them
Without wanting
To pick at their scabs

9.13

From our president
As hurricane Florence
Slowly grinds toward
The outer banks
    3000 people
    Did not die
    In the two hurricanes
    That hit Puerto Rico
    When I left the Island
    AFTER the storm had hit
    They had anywhere
    From 6 to 18 deaths
As time went by
It did not go up
By much
Then, a long time later
They started to report
Really large numbers
Like 3000...
....This was done
By the Democrats
In order to make
Me look

As bad as possible
When I was
Successfully raising
Billions of Dollars
To help rebuild Puerto Rico
If a person died
For any reason
Like old age
Just add them
Onto the list
Bad politics
I love Puerto Rico
@realDonaldTrump
The winds in his skull
Swirl and storm
In their own ecosphere
Of associative timespace

9.14

Rain
60's
Like it has been
All week
I'm making friends
With two young
Female scholars
From China
With Colleen
Drove to Staunton
On Wednesday
For Black Swan Books
Open mic
Last night
Indoor picnic
At EMU
Slowly maybe
Distances shrink
The globe folds
In upon itself

Like a deflated
Beachball
Oceans and eons
Swallowed
The tectonic plates
Of history and culture
Crushed
And our different lives
Exist side by side
We cross through
With talk of children
And books
And American movies
And one of them asks
Do you like Trump?

9.15

Colleen came home
Last night
And told me
She might be offered
A job
Here in this new town
And I wonder
At what point
In the ribbon
Of our adventure
Here
Did someone
Back there
Scissor it in two
And now
Fifty-five years
Of my life
In Texas
Flaps and snaps
In the wind
And I cannot lean
Back far enough

To catch hold
Of it
Without falling

9.16

My girlfriend
In high school
Sat behind me
Last night
In a dream
She is a beautiful
Woman
Now
Still
With eyes
Like those
Of a wise wild animal
Like a mare
Still sleek and strong
She lay her hand
On my shoulder
Leaned toward me
Nuzzled my neck
And whispered
"I am lonely"
Suddenly
I woke
Shaken
And before
I could open
My eyes
I spoke
Into morning
Toward imaginary
Unfenced fields
"I know"

9.17

Yesterday
Cloudy all day
Didn't go to church
I miss it
But don't make
Myself go
Stayed in all day
Out of the grey drizzle
.11 inches yesterday
.14 inches day before
1.299 inches in seven days
3.06 inches this month
11 rain days this month
37.43 inches this year
118 days of rain this year
12 inches above normal
This is not
What I expected
Here
I should be
A frog
A toad
Some in-between character
Adaptable
Ready to leap
Into pools overflowing
But I made
My transition
To upright
Large-brained mammal
Long ago
Or maybe I didn't
I want to make
Some witty comment
Maybe something surreal
Here
At the end
To make a splash
But it's not happening
Oh well

9.19
84 degrees
Sunny
Partly cloudy
I had to squint
While driving
The car
This morning
The sun
Bold exposed
And unexpected
Like your loved one
Stepping out
Of the shower
Whoa
What are you doing
There
You feel embarrassed
For the naked person
But
You'll keep remembering
What they looked like
And wishing
Maybe
Everyday
Could be
The same

9.20
The Supreme Court
MeToo
A Hurricane
And
The Donald talks
Tough times
 I just want to thank
 All the incredible
 Men and women
 Who have done

Such a great job
In helping
With Florence

This is a tough
Hurricane

One of the wettest
We've seen
From the standpoint
Of water

Rarely have we
Had an experience
Like it
And it certainly
Is not good

It's a tough one
Tough to understand
But this has been
A really difficult
Time
For a lot of people

But I really want
To see her
I really would want
To see
What she has to say

But I would say this
I think he is
An extraordinary man
A man of great intellect

A tough one
Tough to understand
As I have been
Telling you

And he has this
Unblemished record

This is a tough thing
For his family
We want to get it
Over with

At the same
Time
We want to give
Tremendous amounts of
Time

This is a tough
Hurricane

If she shows up
That would be
Wonderful
If she doesn't
Show up
That would be
Unfortunate
If she shows up
And makes a credible
Showing
That will be
Very interesting

But it will be
Very hard
For me to imagine
It's a tough one
Tough to understand
But this has been
A really difficult
Time
From the standpoint
Of water

One of the wettest
We've seen
And it certainly
Is not good
At the same
Time
Tough

9.25
When does the rain
End
19 days of rain
This month
5.24 inches of rain
This month
And news continues
To surge
Brett Kavanaugh's
Teenage sex life
Judging the interrupted
Erections
Of a once and future
Yuck
Egotistical
Selfish
Boorish
Privileged
Teen-aged
Prep School
White boy
Emerging
From the swamp
These are the muck creatures
Back-slapping
Keg kids
Self-congratulatory
Boys will be boys
Prima donna
Serial assaulters

Waving their little Eli-s
At astonished girls
Stunned into thirty years
Of agonized silence
Until it thunders
In mediated rage
At outrageous fortune
One woman two women
Maybe a third
When it rains
It cascades
Until he slithers
Maybe
Back into
The flooding murky
Tidal Basin
Waters

9.27
Yesterday
For two hours
Midday
Bright sunshine
85 degrees
Then more rain
Storms and
"cats and dogs"
And on and on
Into this morning
And 58 degrees
A cornfield
On my way to EMU
Shorn and stubbled
The brown ankles
Attentive in rows
Like you know
The shoes
Of murdered children
The puddles

Alive with casings
Of falling rain

9.29
Asheville North Carolina
Colleen and I drove down
Last night
Today late afternoon
I will read poetry
With four others
At a conference celebrating
Black Mountain College
BMC has shadowed
Much of my life
Since undergrad
When my professor
Leonard Lamm
Pointed me toward
Duberman's book
For some reason
I don't remember what
And probably only half read
And then in grad school
New assistant prof
Paul Christensen's
Call Him Ishmael
And somewhere appeared
Creeley Levertov Duncan
And Cage Cunningham Fuller
Jacob Lawrence
Albers and Rauschenberg
MC Richards
And so I feel
Like I am home somehow
Talks on Cage and Dorn
Anis Albers Olsen's letters
And Philip Whalen's journals
I could make a joke
Say that my joy
Marks me a nerd
But why do we
Today
Shame knowledge and
    expertise
In the history of culture
Respect for the pioneers
The real goals
Of a real education
The magnet outside the force
Field of conventional thinking
The hope outside
Of capitalism
Booksales and appearances
On CSpan
Outside of the mass mind
And I begin to think
That maybe I could escape
That maybe I could live
Fulltime in the orbit
Of other suns
Maybe all I need to do
Is retreat into
The forest of language
Of images and significance
Late afternoon I read
Duncan's "A Late Illness"
And my old poem to Duncan
And 9.20
We five poets are here
To celebrate Tom Murphey's
Stone Regna anthology
Hilary Holladay Jeff Davis
Ted Pope and Tom
It's a good reading
For the few who have
    remained
For our late hour
We are all here as children
Of Black Mountain

We are all here
Because a good college
Is an idea
And a good idea always
Has students and teachers

October

10.4
That moment
One hour into
On a crowded airplane
30,000 feet above ground
Clouds so thick below you
So you can see nothing
To touch down upon
And the young woman
Beside you
Blue jean jacket green jeans
And white flipflops
Long black hair
Fluffing down her back
Has not stopped talking
To her two friends across
The aisle
And you think
When will the man
With the cart full
Of those little bottles
Of booze
Get here
And intercede
In her monologue
With those cheerful words
"Anything for you, sir?"
And you will say
Yes bourbon please
And a cup of silence

10.9
Dear Lyman
   During the budgeting review,
   it was brought to my attention
   that we have overpaid you for work year to date.

I know how it happened,
but that doesn't help
matters on your end.

I would like to spend
some time talking through
the details and work out
a plan going forward.
What time works
best for you?

Current Overpayment:
$4,542.27

Possible Next Steps:
1. Discontinue the payments for tutoring for October – December, 2018
2. Decreasing your current payments for tutoring and spread out the overpayment over additional months.
3. Other suggestions?

10.10
Another lightly raining day
My mother's birthday
She would be nearing
One hundred
A few years left to go
But already
She has been dead
Longer
Than she was alive
That idea makes the nerves
Go zip and fizzle
I've been hiding

From this book
Here at the turn
Into fall
Too many essays
To grade
Too many grad students
To talk to
Too much traveling
To Asheville
(Was that only
Two weeks ago)
To Austin
For another reading
With five friends
And our anthology
And seeing William and Kati
I am now so far behind
With my paid work
And of course
Kavanaugh was approved
That little storm is over
Like so many storms
This year
They come and go
And now Michael
Is pounding
The Florida coast
And I have been hiding
In a word game on my phone
Assign me letters
And crossword me
Into frustration
"Never a cross word"
In the *lab*
Each bleach will *leach*
And *lace*
To *heal* with *ale*
Hey *hale Ace cable*
The *cab* to the *beach*
Bale while you're *able*

The basic components
Of poetry laid out
Just vowels and consonants
In consonance
How many times
Has that one been said
Nothing is new
Except what is
Level 162 down and done
Now level 163
And it's getting damned
Difficult
I look at the letters
And say WTF
I like the word
Purty
Like my mother
Might say
But the snotty
Nose in the air
Game won't accept it
A *trip* to the *yurt* is a *pity*
Pry the *pit*
To *put* in a *tip*
Try and *rip*
Get out of the *rut*
And find the word
That holds
All the other words
The word source
The mother word
"In motherwords"
This time is *purity*
Songs and dances
From my "device"
Next level 164
And the source
Easy to see
Is *yearly*
Dis-member it

Lyman Grant

And re-member
Eleven more words
Remember
The *early year*
1969 and my mother
In her last bed
It's a bad blast
Blessed
And she's dead
How many words
Can cancer ransom

10.11
Kanye West and
Jim Brown visit
Donald Trump
In the Oval Office
To discuss
Important matters
And have lunch

    What people don't know
    Everyone knows

    Never thought about it
    I like North Korea

    It was so close
    I don't say anything is
      solved
    It was a big solving
    And not solved yet

    It's the bravery that helps
    You beat this game called
      life
    This hat it gave me power
    "I am with her"
    Didn't make me feel

As a guy
Male energy going on
You made a superman
Put the beep on it
I have enough balls
They didn't teach us
Mental health makes
Us do crazy things
The trap door
The 13th amendment
It was illegal
For blacks to read
If you read the amendment
You would get locked up
And turned into a slave
We don't need sentences
He looked at my brain
It's equal in three parts
I am going to drop
Some bombs on you
We need pardons
We just say positive
Lovely divine
Universal words

Jim do you want
To say something

It doesn't look good
We don't look good
Makes a lot of sense

That was quite something
That was quite something

I just channeled it
I don't answer questions
In simple soundbites
You are tasting a fine wine
It is multiple notes

I'm open-minded
I'm here

All we really have
Is today
Over and over
And over again
The eternal return
The hero's journey
And Trump is on
His hero's journey
He might not have expected
To have a crazy
motherfucker

Let me ask you this
    question
How does it feel
To be in the Oval Office
Isn't it good energy
Jim how do you feel

I feel good
I truly feel good

It was set up
To be a lunch
Of two people
That I like
And I guess they like me
I had important meetings
    today
With senators and
    everything
Nobody cared

10.13
I keep thinking
That at some moment

The sky will splinter
And the nail of sunshine
Will pierce the gloom

10.14
Log by log
I have broken
The dam
Of grading
Through
A weekend's
Devotion
To student poems
Rather than
The growing panic
Of mute anticipation
Rising backstream
Now the clear
Current
Passes steady
Within banks
The lumber
Of community
Flowing down stream
Milled
And graded
Employed
In building
The future
Church
Of language

10.15
The drive to work
Behind a semi-truck
Small metal cages
Stacked eight tall
Filled with bundles

Of white feathers
Like bouquets
Tossed abandoned
At the stoplight
Tiny heads rise
And gaze
In silence

The drive home
After work
Behind another
Semi
Small metal cages
Stacked eight tall
Filled with evening
Light and shadow
Rinsed of white fallings
Like magnolia petals
The wind
And the silence

10.16
I should mention
That two weeks ago
I visited Austin
Checked out
Our house there
Our trailer there
Checked in with
My son and his wife there
My friends Dreux
Charlotte Rick Talbot
Aimee her daughter Terra
There
Read poems
With John Bill
David John
At Malvern Book Store
Launching

Our anthology
Five Friends
Sunday Afternoons
There
There were over
Fifty people
There
In the audience
Listening to us
Read our poems
There
In the audience
Were Prudence Lisa
Richard Kathrine
Rich Heloise
William Kati
Two of my online
Poetry students
A cute ten-year old boy
We all signed a book for
They were all
There
And now
Two weeks later
Colleen at work
Theo at school
I am alone
In the dining room
Writing about it
Here

10.17
Our president
Just called a woman
He once
Hardened himself
For sex with
"Horseface"
As he jumped

Between the sheets
With ruthless
Crown Prince
Mohammed bin Salman
Son of King Salman
Of Saudi Arabia
Who ordered
Journalist Jamal Khashoggi
Murdered
Call this poem
"Bed-Time"

10.18
It is with great sadness
And reluctance
That I tell you
I am resigning
From my job
At the end
Of the semester

I want you to know
I thoroughly enjoy
My work as a tutor
And believe
I have done some good
Work with several students
I have great respect
For you and the college
The teacher/lover of language
Part of me
Does not want to resign
However
I am having health issues
Sitting in a chair
18 hours a week
Has been taking a toll
On my back
Over the past year

Even with chiropractic help
And physical therapy
My symptoms continue
to deteriorate
Recently I had an MRI
Next week
I will begin steroid injections
And I assume
I will require back surgery
Early next year

While the recent confusion
Over my compensation
Is not the reason
For my resigning
I do have to say
It is a factor
Making the decision
Less difficult
The prospect
Of "paying back the college"
Several thousand dollars
Because somehow
The college placed
Me on a pay scale
Incorrectly is
To say the least
Troubling

I am very appreciative
Of the opportunity
To be part
Of the EMU community
This year
I wish
It could have been
Longer

Respectfully,
Lyman

10.19
    Dear Lyman
    I have received a response
    from the Provost
    He has agreed to not go
        back
    on the incorrect amount.
    We will make the change
    for October 1 and following
    to go to the correct salary
        amount
    Please let me know
    if you still want to meet
    so that I can review
    everything with you.

10.22
Tonight
Shenandoah Valley
The first chill
The smudge of distant
Dark mountains
On low horizon
Almost a full
Dollop of moon
Daubed upon clear sky
A spoonful of cream
Spilled upon a navy
Black table cloth
And hung outside
The window

Quiet night
Fireplace hiss and wave
Rest after
Three and half day
Trip to Birmingham
And back
To see college boy
For parent's weekend
This time
Could not make it
To Kelly Ingram Park
As I wanted
So I would have something
To write about
Something "liberal"
Something thematic
For the fourth quarter
Of this book
That place
Called
"A place of reconciliation
And revolution"
We've been there
Before
Walked the paths
Stood among
Barking dogs
Their iron teeth
Water hoses
Soaked by shame
Shook with horror
Outside the 16th Street
Baptist Church
Wept and ascended
With the doves
Carol Denise McNair
Addie Mae Collins
Cynthia Wesley
Carole Robertson
Say their names
Don't breeze over them
Every time
I return
To my old home town
A part of me is there
Not over the mountain
Where I grew up

Segregated
And ignorant
"Protected"
And proud
But walking
That city block
Catching maybe
Intimations
Glimpses of four men
Dark night shadows
Placing dynamite
And a cheap timer
Under the church steps
Proud white men
Smiling at imminent murder
Happy with
Their imagined debris
In history

But this time
A day and a half
With my son Jacob
Celebrating homecoming
Food trucks on the quad
The young men and
Their parents at the frat house
Volleyball games
Dinner with his friends
Boujee tacos
Ice cream and
College boy stories
A night peaceful
Over the mountain
Yet somehow always haunted

10.23
And now this rattles
Around in cable news
    A globalist is a person
that wants the globe
to do well,
frankly, not caring
about our country
so much.
And you know
what?
We can't have
that.
You know,
they have a word.
It sort of became
old-fashioned.
It's called a nationalist.
And I say, really,
we're not supposed
to use that word.
You know what
I am?
I'm a nationalist,
OK?
I'm a nationalist.

10.24
Morning drive
Theo's school
Then my school
33 degrees
Will have to begin
Parking car in garage
Next week

Morning classes
With my presentation
On presentations
Due next week
A little po-mo
Meta fun
That maybe only I

Will get caught
Inside of

After classes
News of pipe bombs
To Clinton Obama
Brennan Holder
Waters Soros
No explosions
Except on cable
Breaking News

How does one receive
This information
Hoax incompetence
Revolution counter revolution
Outrage shame
Fear detachment
By keeping to one's aisle
At Friendly's Food Co-op
Baguettes and Brie
And the daily soup
Would anyone notice me
At Ace Hardware
Cart stocked with
Wires batteries pvc bb's
Digital clocks
Set at 0 hour
Is this the way
The world begins
To end
Not with a bang
But a fizzle

But what I want
To remember
Are the clouds
This morning
Over the eastern mountains
The sun still hiding

But tinting
The underbellies
Of mauve clouds
In pink
Like warm coals under ash
Oven mitts tindered
Lifted from stove flame
Strawberries
In blue milk
An old man's face
Slapped
Smudged blood
On cotton balls
Rose petals
A lover's back
Musked tussled sheets
And morning peeking

10.25
So on Facebook
All my poet Friends
Are mourning
The death
Of Tony Hoagland
At 64
Ha I think
I outlived him
Ha I think
Now we know
That irony
Does not prevent
Or cure
Cancer
They add hearts
Meaning "love"
And faces with tears
Meaning "sadness"
And thumbs up
Meaning "like"

That one confuses
Even me
But ha
I think
Maybe now
I will be able
To write a poem
Better than he
Wrote
Has written
Is done writing
At least he won't
Write any more
Poems
Better than
My poems
Then ha I think
Maybe
I am still getting
The whole thing
Wrong
Every photo
I see
Of Tony Hoagland
Shows him
Smiling
Like big broad
Shit eating grins
Damn I think
Good job
Tony

10.30
Bright Sun
Chilled
Feeling like I ought to
Feeling like I should stop
My life
And take notice

Here again
That 14 pipe bombs
Were sent
Last week
To 12 men and women
Who represent
Democratic values
And
Opposition to white
People's terrorism
Every one intercepted
Every one unexploding
Luck ignorance
Stupid coup
Clever hoax
I do not know
I do know
That I feel no poetry
Here
Nor
In the deaths
Of two African American
Elders
In Kentucky
Nor
In the murder
Of eleven members
Of Tree of Life
Synagogue
In Pittsburgh
What is it
Am I just too numb
Now
We live our lives
For a few weeks
And then
We are attacked
One of us
Some of us
Some crazy guy

Decides that his hate
In more glorious
Than our tedious joy
This past week
I welcomed a steroid
Shot in my spine
I tried to rest
And let it take effect
I drove Theo
To a high school dance
I graded student work
I drove to Richmond
For a chance to see
Fall's glorious color
I test drove
Four automobiles
A new hybrid
Excited me
This was my dull
Ordinary life
Like the life
Of Maurice Stallard
Taking his grandson
To Kroger's
To purchase poster board
For a school project
Like the life
Of Rose Mallinger
Bubbie
Grandmother
Worshipping
Saturday morning
At her synagogue
As she had
Unharmed
For sixty years

He says hyperbolically
   My eyes
   are now wide open
   and now realize
   I've been used to
   spread messages
   I don't believe in.
   I am distancing myself
   from politics
   and completely
   focusing on being
   creative !!!
   @kanyewest
Can one be
Creative
Without focusing
On the politics
Of being
Creative???

10.31
Boo!
Yesterday's big news

November

11.1
Dawning ocean sky
Clear aqua and coral clouds
My morning plunge

11.4
Sunday
Pretty day
Inside
Making things orderly
Making piles disappear
Grading virtual stacks online
Presentations on Luther
Michelangleo Vico Bernini
Newton Machiavelli
Something maybe
They won't forget
No matter who/what
They become

Afternoon five friends
Writing group
Somehow the prompt
That catches spark
Is "bonfires"

What do you want
To do
Now that the alarm
Is ringing
In the next room
You're going to have to get up
Walk down the hall
And by yourself
Make the silence you need
It's really not
Such a bad thing
To be reminded that time
Is passing

Maybe even running out
The dripping faucet
The creek out back in summer
Will these things
Always keep running
You know the feeling so well
The two-lane at 11:00
The moon out front
High and far away
And the road
(Does it go on forever)
How far did you really want
To drive that day
This day
Ever
And back home
Remember home
That room
Down the hall
Where the bell is clanging
It contains your life
Savings
Treasures clippings photos
Letters mementos junk
You realize
Collecting
Was your life's work
Doing things
Only because you wanted
A memory of it
Collecting relics
Of your own sacred life
And now
That bell's still ringing
And you imagine
All this debris
The clutter
Of your one life
In the pasture
Behind the house

In flames

11.6
The evening
Ritual
Dusk fall chill
Dog sniffing
Gold dead leaves
And ghost whiffs
Of landscape's
Migrant
History
In scent loss
Here his piss
There his shit
Then dinner
Empty bowl
Suddenly
Full again

In
One hour
Polls will close
And ballots
Will be raked
Together
And counted
T.V.'s snout
Tabulates
The fragrant
Fading trails
Of our redolent
Republic

11.7
The proverbial glass
In every citizen's hand
Here 49% empty
There 51% full
There 51% empty
Here 49% full
And we all cry
Over spilled milk

11.8
You can't even
Sculpt an opinion
Worth sharing
About Trump's firing
The Attorney General
Before
News breaks
That twelve
More have bled
From a lone
Gunman
In California

11.11
Frying bacon
In cast iron skillet
Standing at kitchen window
Watching leaves descend
Like memories neglected
Like promises broken
This windless morning
For no reason
Other than it is time
Stabbing slices of meat
Turning them over
In sizzle fat smoking
Sipping my coffee
And the leaves sway
Like glinting coins
Falling
In a wishing well

A dance
A swirl of hips
A hand reaching out
An invitation
A memorial
A whirl of gratitude
And winter's peace
Announced
Upon this ground
The drench
Of *Ginko's*
Lemon leaves
In grass
Like pooled golden blood
Of the slain

11.15
In the house
The fireplace warm
Strong dark coffee
From the French press
Tears from the baguette
Butter and blackberry jam
From a local farm
Early snow and
School's closed
Yes it is as cozy
As your imagination
Will allow you
To make it

But
Today
This
From our president
   The White House
   is running
   very smoothly
   and the results
for our Nation
are obviously very good.
We are the envy
of the world.
But anytime
I even think
about making changes,
the FAKE NEWS MEDIA
goes crazy,
always seeking
to make us look
as bad as possible!
Very dishonest!
Then
   The inner workings
   of the Mueller
   investigation
   are a total mess.
   They have found
   no collusion
   and have gone
   absolutely nuts.
   They are screaming
   and shouting at people,
   horribly
   threatening them
   to come up
   with the answers
   they want.
   They are
   a disgrace
   to our Nation
   and don't...
   ....care
   how many lives
   the [sic] ruin.
   These are Angry People,
   including the highly
   conflicted Bob Mueller,
   who worked

>   for Obama
>   for 8 years.
>   They won't even look
>   at all of the bad acts
>   and crimes
>   on the other side.
>   A TOTAL
>   WITCH HUNT
>   LIKE NO OTHER
>   IN AMERICAN
>   HISTORY!
> Then
>   Universities
>   will someday study
>   what highly conflicted
>   (and NOT Senate
>   approved)
>   Bob Mueller and his gang
>   of Democrat thugs
>   have done
>   to destroy people.
>   Why is he protecting
>   Crooked Hillary,
>   Comey, McCabe, Lisa Page
>   & her lover, Peter S,
>   and all of his friends
>   on the other side?
> Then
>   The only "Collusion"
>   is that of the Democrats
>   with Russia
>   and many others.
>   Why didn't the FBI
>   take the Server
>   from the DNC?
>   They still don't have it.
>   Check out
>   how biased Facebook,
>   Google and Twitter
>   are in favor
>   of the Democrats.
>   That's the real Collusion!
>   @realDonaldTrump

And I think
I will not let
This imbecile
Ruin this day
The coffee is bitter
But I am not
The bread is crusty
But I am not
The butter is hard
But I am not
The jam is seedy
But I am not
I am
Eager for the beauty
Of this day
Thirsty and hungry
The plate of morning
Set before me
I can take it in
And let it nourish me

11.16

Autumn leaves
Fallen upon ice
Stained as if stabbed
By shards of glass

11.17

Two days of reading
And marking
My freshmen's
Researched essays
Almost final drafts
If I wish to be sullen

I could be
Is APA really that difficult
Is a thesis sentence
That does more than name
And enumerate
Really such a foreign concept
Do they really think
I cannot tell a 16-point
Typeface
From the required 12-point
But I am not
My frustrations
Are like ice
Hard and cold
Until the light broadens
And the winds warm
Now drinking de-caf
In Barnes and Noble
Just to have something
Different to look at
Before I write
The last evaluation
For this set of drafts
And hope
That the final drafts
On Monday
Reflect our efforts
I refresh the chilled
Waters of style
With random sips
And dips
Into the new
Ah!
Here
Jon Meacham
Splashes upon me
   The good news
   Is that we have
   Come through
   Such darkness

Before

11.18
I live
2697 miles
From Paradise
California
Google tells me
I am
1 day and 15 hours
Away
If I drive without stopping
If I did
When I arrived
I would not find
Paradise
Unless one thinks
That Paradise
Is 14,000 burned out houses
Instead I watch
The videos on YouTube
Of the Camp Fire
And of the Woolsey Fire
North of Malibu
Parents singing
To their children
And the walls of flame
Stretching out
Fingers of fire
Blazing stalks spitting embers
Crimson teeth
Caught in the currents
And the child begging
Are we going to die
The parent maybe making
One last lie
Every promise
Is a prayer
How can it be

A traffic jam leaving
Paradise
Automobiles stalled
And abandoned
A neighbor frantic
Breathless sprinting
Through the midnight
Dark smoke of that terrible
Morning
And
There I was
Last night
In the auditorium at EMU
Watching listening
To students
In their end
Of semester gala
Playing Bernstein Merchant
Holsinger Mussorgsky
And concluding
With Faure's *Requiem*
And that is why
I woke up thinking
About Paradise
   Requiem aeternam....
   Kyrie eleison
   Christe eleison
Over seventy have died
Maybe a thousand missing
   Free the souls
   Of the dead
   From the punishment
   Of hell
   And the deep pit...

   ...Into paradise
   May angels draw them
   On your arrival
   May the martyrs receive
   You and lead you into the
   holy city

11.25
Lying in bed
Last night
Thinking
I had not added
To this thing
For several days
I tried to think
About what
I would add
I suspect
You are tired
Of hearing about
My busy days
The grading
I am tired
Of writing
About that
Also
So enough
For now
I thought about
The drive
From my sister's
Yesterday
After Thanksgiving
With family
Rain all the way
Cold
The trees leafless
The gray wet
For five hours
There is
Something there
I can't
Quite get to
The way limbs

Reach
Like fingers
Naked wet
Into the dull
Bare air
Like hands
Without
Their green mittens
Each twig
Each branch
Each tree
In its own rain
I know that
Shiver
That merely my-
Self desire
The necessity
To pull tight
Into oneself
To encase
To glaze over
And wait
And wait
And anyway
This is not
The poem
I wrote
Last night
In my head
Lying in bed
Thinking I should
Get up
And write it down
But today
I remembered
That I was remembering
The trees
I thought then
They might be
Beautiful

But
There is this poem
Instead

11.27
My poet friends in Austin
The ones I meet with some
    Sundays
Through video sometimes worry
    about
What a poem actually is
And whether they are actually
Writing poems or something else
Something shamefully lesser
You can tell I don't worry
About that these days at least
Not in exactly the same way
They are worrying over it
I began this year reading A.R.
Ammons' tape spooling into
The year and Ammons' negligent
Poetics gave me the permission
I was needing but even he would
Worry over this big question
About what it is when we
Commit ourselves to
    communing
With language and listening to it
And trying to find a freedom
For ourselves by caging wild
    words
Of course most folks don't look
At it that way even Ammons
    spoke
About the Muse waiting on the
    Muse
Enticing the Muse where the
    fuck
Is the Muse where did she go

wondering
Off to what the hell does the Muse want
From us like all we poets ever do
Is speak softly begging over and over
Every day and night pitifully
Like a groom urging his nervous
Virgin bride out of the bathroom
Or maybe it is that we are shocked
When the Muse shows up in the kitchen
Naked and there we are all grimy
From working on the car in the garage
And wow really now she is ready
And anyway that metaphor seems
So stupidly patriarchal these days
So what is it we do and how do
We know if we are doing it well
I think I have quit asking those questions
Not because I do not believe that
There are better or lesser poems
And that there are not poets better
Than I am geez wouldn't that be
A silly thing to say at this point
In this year with this project coming
To an end and if you have read this far
And you having come to some sort
Of conclusion about your wasted time
Or not it is just that this is what I do
And I am attempting to do it well
To have a little fun along the way
To use the knowledge that I have
Some tricks I have seen others use
And never ceasing to believe
That I am living my life as if it
Were a poem that there is poetry
All around me if I would just
Wake up and see it hear it and then
Write it down and for me to write
This year down without the fuss
Of trying so show off unless
Somehow showing off seemed to be
The exact right thing to be doing then
Now the truth is I have to go to work
Right now I am running kind of late

11.28
So the thing
On the television
Now
Is that today
Is the day
That the end
Of Trump
Began
Manafort's deal
Revoked
Because his lawyers
Have been feeding
Trump's lawyers
Tiny morsels
Of delicious information
Somebody's getting fat
Wonder who
And Cohen's deal
Is secured
Both label someone
Individual # 1
Wonder who

Maybe it's
A good day
Everything's gonna be
Okay
But I won't listen
To what they say
Until Individual # 1
Is put away
Then we'll all have
A partay
On the Jersey Shore
Shooting AK
I'll buy Colleen
A bouquet
We'll cook a dinner
Gourmet
And we'll all sing
Hooray
And that will be
A good day
Let us pray

December

12.4
So there's a lunatic
In a big house
Dining with our future's
　tableware
Denying the conspiracy
Of everyone's imagination
And there's a dead man
Boxed beautifully
On his way to light
The eternal flame
Deaf to the orators
In their busy black suits
Reading his cold noble lips
Praising the pungent
　commentary
Of his peculiar stockings
And there's us
Hymning the never-ending
Dirge of charge card
Hypocrisies and our politics
Going (baby) boom

12.5
A beautiful day
30-degree morning
Snowfall
While driving Theo to school
And me to work
By the end of the class hour
Out the window
Cotton fluff on bare branches
Brown grass painted pure
The stillness
Except
Hunched students
Kokopellis with purpose
Trudging the final weeks'
　dance
Who has eyes ears
Available for astonishment
Who will remove
Their flute
Whose chilled fingers
Will hunt
For the elusive melody
Of useless wonder

12.6
Can I say
I did not want
To do this one
Beat about the Bushes
Either one
I have never been
A fan
Though they seem
Likeable enough
In person
In imagination
Cold martinis
Adirondacks
Staring at the endless
Blue ocean
Remembering walls
And towers falling

Today there is always
The sense that always
Is no more
The beast slouching
Courting readerlessness
The carelessness
Of the inarticulate
The heartlessness
Of incompetent wrath
Jon Meacham remembers
　His life code,
　as he said,

was "Tell the truth.
Don't blame people.
Be strong.
Do your best.
Try hard.
Forgive.
Stay the course."
And that was and is
the most American of
   creeds.
Abraham Lincoln's
"better angels of our nature"
and George H.W. Bush's
"thousand points of light"
are companion verses
in America's national hymn.
Somewhere in the Cathedral
Inside a hollow chest sings
   We are going to win
   like we've never won before.
   Like we've never won
      before.
   Because we are finally
   putting America first.
   We're putting America first.
   And by the way,
   you know
   all the rhetoric you see,
   the Thousand Points of
      Light.
   What the hell
   was that by the way?
   Thousands Points of Light.
   What did that mean?
   Does anyone know?
   Has anyone ever
   figured that one out?
And yes a pal a chum a friend
Had "figured it out"
   And he was a man
of such great humility,
those who travel
the high road of humility
in Washington, D.C.,
are not bothered
by heavy traffic.
And somewhere down below
In the valley
An unpredictable driver
Hair tussled in the wind
Follows his own personal GPS
Into another dead end
   We are all going
   to the same place
   Probably one or
   two places
   you know
   But we are all
   the same
   And I do have
   much more humility
   Than a lot of people
   would think
A son
And imperfect son
Honors his father
Becomes
Now the father
Figures it took this long
Maybe now more the man
We all wanted him
To be
Before he hitched to Cheney
   Dad taught us
   that public service
   is noble and necessary;
   that one can serve
   with integrity
   and hold true
   to the important values,

like faith and family.
He strongly believed
that it was important
to give back
to the community and
    country
in which one lived.
He recognized
that serving others
enriched the giver's soul.
To us, his was the brightest
of a thousand points of
    light.
And arms crossed
Sullen and confused
Golden haired
Dreams again
Of great moments
In a life gifted
With his own kind
Of faith and family
    I moved on her, actually.
    You know, she was down
    on Palm Beach.
    I moved on her,
    and I failed.
    I'll admit it.
    I did try and fuck her.
    She was married.
    I moved on her like a bitch.
    But I couldn't get there.
    And she was married.
    Then all of a sudden
    I see her,
    she's now got
    the big phony tits
    and everything.
    She's totally changed her
        look.
    Yeah, that's her.
    With the gold.
    I better use some Tic Tacs
    just in case I start kissing
    her.
    You know,
    I'm automatically attracted
    To beautiful —
    I just start kissing them.
    It's like a magnet.
    Just kiss.
    I don't even wait.
    And when you're a star,
    they let you do it.
    You can do anything.
    Grab 'em by the pussy.
    You can do anything.
Billy was a Bush
He had time for
Could understand
Man to man
Those were the days

12.7
It's been a week
Of filings
Of scrapings
Of frictions
Cohen Manafort Flynn
There is a sense
That Mueller is courting us
In negative space
█████████████
Documenting not
In black letters
But in strips of emptiness
█████████████
The abyss a nation stares into
And sees itself
Redacted

Erased

Meanwhile

Tillerson talked
To Trump of
Mere matters of state
    We did not have
    A common value system
    He'd say here's what I want
    To do and here's how
    I want to do it
    And I'd have to say
    I understand
    What you want to do
    But you can't do it that way
    Because it violates the law.
    It violates a treaty.
[The moron is]
He says
    A man who is pretty
    Undisciplined
    Doesn't like to read
    Doesn't read briefing
       reports
    Doesn't like
    To get into the details
    Of a lot of things
    But rather says
    This is what I believe
Trump tweets his own desolate
    beliefs
In sophomore similes
The Boy Scout he says
    Is dumb as a rock
As empty as a sock
With a hole in it
    I couldn't get rid
    Of him
    Fast enough

Trump had to be tough
He ended
It in a tweet he did
    He was lazy as hell
Trump would tell him
What he wanted to do
Rex would say screw
You and your hotels
    Now it's a whole new
    Ball game
Nothing's the same
    Great spirit at State
Wishes he could eliminate it
He'll just decimate it
Meanwhile we can
    contemplate
How Trump is dumb as hell
And as lazy as a rock
The great spirit states
The ball game is new
Could we not fast enough
Get rid of him

12.8
They are beginning
To talk
About the end
Of the year
And the contributions
I could make
If I only act
Now

Soon
That will pass
And then
The wrap-ups
Will begin
The top ten

The best of
The sorry
You missed its

And
I am beginning
To feel
That the end
Of this book
Is winking
At me

Telling me
The end is
Revealing itself
Like an old
Man pulling down
His shorts
To show me
His ass

Or
Has the year
Which began
Nude and happy
Like a newborn
Smiling
In the crib
Finally
Dressed itself
And is walking
Out the door

12.9
Sunday night after watching
Captain America: Civil War
With Theo and Colleen
It's been a quiet slow day
Some early morning errands

And breakfast at Waffle House
Snow light and tender
    asauntering
From noon gray skies into
    darkness
Profligating my time as if piles
Of it were carelessly raked
Like hay in a painting by Millet
I assume they are all still talking
On the television about the thing
That they are all talking about
All their talk is going to continue
Just like that they talk about the
    things
That all of them are talking about
And then something happens and
Boom they change the thing they
    are
Talking about to the new thing
To talk about it is that simple
Really
    And it struck me
That there are all sorts of things
That we were talking about once
And are no longer talking about
In a way this book is a record
Of the things that we stopped
Talking about does that kind
Of thing happen in our real lives
Sometime this year my back
Really did hurt I went to PT
And not much came from that
    then
I met with a doctor and the
    doctor
Shot steroids into my spine and
I think didn't I stop writing about
My back I didn't even mention
That I got a second shot last week
But my back is still a thing I

think
About things come and go and
    they don't
Really go away do they and by
    the way
I have not eaten any chips
    since
The middle of July this is a big
    deal
For a chubby guy like me now
I have to work on baked goods
Like muffins cookies but this is
    something
I haven't talked about I am
    wondering
About those kids from
    Parkland
I heard donations are down
At the NRA and that their
    candidates
Lost in November I am
    wondering
About the kids along the
    border
And their mothers and fathers
I think about #metoo what are
    all
Those guys up to now how
    distant
Is justice do the women think
    what
Are they doing with their lives
    the wheels
Of indifference just keep on
    rolling
I am wondering about Puerto
    Rico
And their recovery and North
    Carolina and Florence and
    Florida
And Michael the fires in
    California
McCain and Bush the drama
And the new drama Stormy
    Daniels
Now owes $300,000 to
    Trump's
Lawyers shouldn't we try to
    regather
To try to understand or is our
    life
These days just a walk in a
    snowy
Field we leave our prints and
It is a slow day nothing hurries
But the prints eventually
    disappear
If we wait patiently enough a
    new
Snow will blow in and we'll be
    fine
Oh yeah Stan Lee died too
    some time ago

12.11

The moon sleeps
In an orange hammock
In the southwestern sky

12.12

Pavements smirk
Their dull proud-
Plowedness
Sidewalks flirt
Part shoveled
And bare
Part covered
In icy-

Stubbornness
Snow gathers
Piled at street corners
Its stained
Unkempt innocence
Taunting

12.14
Even though
I have three sets
Of essays
One set
Of poetry portfolios
To read and grade
And 18 hours
More next week
Tutoring grad students
With extensions
I feel free
Today
As I were some bouncer
And opened a door
Shoving
All the clouds
Out of the way
And the sun
Has come striding
Through
Warming and brightening
This otherwise
Cold and dreary day
All so I can turn
Tomorrow
And reenter
The dark loud
Drunken jangle

12.17
This late afternoon
Achilled in bright irony
After a half-panicked
Day of marking and editing
Computing grades
I mean like all day
Nose and pencil grinding
Get those final grades
Into the computer system
Don't be late
A big bull of a guy
Coughs his way
Into a tutoring session
Good God I thought
Here it comes
The miserable phlegm
Of my holiday season
And a happy infected
New Year to you too sir
And I thought
If only clarity and economy
Were as contagious
As whatever he was hacking

Behind him
Through the window
I see the sun take to its bed
With a hot toddy
And a box of pick tissues

12.19
All done
You won't have to listen
To me go on
About grading or
Sitting in an office
Helping adults wrestle
The English language

Carpet burns from
Pinning down a run-on
Sore tendons from
Strong-arming transitions
Into logical alignment
Silent night
Jingle bells
Deck the halls
I am done

12.20
A news story
Just reminded me
That in 2018
Because I am White
I could
    Ask for directions
    Redeem a coupon
    Help a homeless man
    Campaign door to door
    Golf slowly
    Wait for a friend in a coffee
      shop
    Swim in a pool
    Barbecue in a park
    Operate a lemonade stand
    Eat lunch on a college
      campus
    Nap in my university's
      common room
    Work out at a gym
    Work as a home inspector
    Move into an apartment
    Mow the wrong lawn
    Not wave while leaving an
      Airbnb
    Work as a firefighter
    Drive with leaves on my car
    Deliver newspapers
    Shop for prom clothes
    Sell a bottle of water on a
      sidewalk
    Ride in a car with
      my White grandmother
    Babysit two White children
    Wear a backpack
    And accidentally brush
      against a woman
    Shop while pregnant
Without inspiring
Some concerned White citizen
To call the police
Doesn't seem like these acts
Are a such big deal
But White paranoia doesn't
Really chew on me does it
Except maybe as an acid
That eats at the soul
Of this nation everyday
And regularly vomits itself
Upon me and my indifference

12.21
Rainy and cold
For some reason
I think of Longfellow
Now you, O sinking
Ship of State!
Bail on, Republic,
Strong and great!
Thy citizens
With all their fears,
Are losing hopes
For future years,
They worry breathless
Of thy fate!
We know that Mattis
Held thy keel,

His backbone wrought
With rods of steel,
But Trump has seized
Thy sail, and rope,
What chaos rings,
What dangers beat,
In what a forge
And what a heat
Do he and Putin
Smash our hope!
Fear, fear each sudden
News bite shock,
'Tis is a wave
And is a rock;
It is the rending
Of the sail,
When Giuliani
Does regale!
In spite of FOX
And fake news roar,
In spite of Hannity,
The bore,
Bail on, Trump wants
The wall, you see!
Our hearts, our hopes,
The refugees
Have earned much more,
Our prayers, our tears.
Our faith triumphant
O'er our fears,
Are all with Mueller,
Yes, praise be!

12.22
Shut your mouth
Shut the door
Shutter speed
Shut 'er down

12.24
So let's imagine
The improbable
Let's say that someone
Reads this book
In 50 years 100 years
A single volume
In a post-apocalyptic
Ruined bookstore
With cancerous rats
And wild dogs
With ringworm and mange
The last book
About to make
A little fire
Or on a more hopeful note
One book among many
Belonging to a happy
Collector who purchased
This book this thing
In a small bookstore
And shelved it
Among favorites
Only to be discovered
(Not a great word for
A book: dis-covered)
By the great grandchildren
(who don't even care for
The concept of covers
Because they have never
Fondled a book
As a manual object)
When cleaning out
The library of their great
Grandparents' McMansion
When they spread the book
Open will the first thing
They notice
Be that the most important
Event of the year

Was not mentioned
Like finding poems
From 1929
And not seeing a line
About Oct 29

Just in case

Trump is still
Wildly reacting
Careening public policy
As if the nation were
A pinball machine
And he madly
Commanding the flippers
Dangerously flirting
with TILT

    To those few Senators
    who think I don't like
    or appreciate being allied
    with other countries,
    they are wrong,
    I DO.
    What I don't like,
    however,
    is when many
    of these same countries
    take advantage
    of their friendship
    with the United States,
    both in Military Protection
    and Trade...
    @realDonaldTrump
    6:41am

    ....We are substantially
    subsidizing the Militaries
    of many VERY rich
        countries
    all over the world,
    while at the same time
    these countries take
    total advantage
    of the U.S.,
    and our TAXPAYERS,
    on Trade.
    General Mattis
    did not see this as a
        problem.
    I DO,
    and it is being fixed!
    @realDonaldTrump
    6:59am

    The only problem
    our economy has
    is the Fed.
    They don't have a feel
    for the Market,
    they don't understand
    necessary Trade Wars
    or Strong Dollars
    or even Democrat
        Shutdowns
    over Borders.
    The Fed is
    like a powerful golfer
    who can't score
    because he has no touch
    - he can't putt!
    @realDonaldTrump
    7:55am

I wonder if we are tired
Of winning yet
Dow 1.2.18=24,824.01
Dow 10.3.18=26,828.29
Dow 12.24.18=21.729.20

Trump is
Like a starting pitcher
Lots of stuff
For five innings
Then the batters
Begin blasting him
No staying power

   I am all alone
   (poor me)
   in the White House
   waiting
   for the Democrats
   to come back
   and make a deal
   on desperately
   needed Border Security.
   At some point
   the Democrats
   not wanting to make a deal
   will cost our Country
   more money
   than the Border Wall
   we are all talking about.
   Crazy!
   @realDonaldTrump
   9:29am

What will it be
That future
Decides
Defines
What
This year
Was

12.25
This morning
Lightened/lighted
By Wendell Berry's
Christmas tree
Without lights
   (we have had enough
   of little lights/
   calling attention
   to themselves)
Re-minding me
That Christ has come
Into the world
And that whether
I know this
Or believe this
(Fake fact?)
I can be mind-ful
Of the Christ-Idea
An old and patient love
Nurtured in acts
As selfless
As humus
As tender
As pine perfume

12.29
Warmish day
Mid-fifties
Pittsboro North Carolina
11:28pm
I thought
I should write something
I am running out
Of time
Colleen and I are here
A straight four-hour drive
Because she wanted
To attend a fancy tea
With my sister nieces
And great nieces
Little sandwiches

Cookies sweets
Tea in China
With flowers and birds
Clemson won
Alabama won
In spite of a wee bit
Of Jameson's
I can't sleep
I have been reading
Zealot by Reza Aslan
Because I think
Next year I want
To study the gospels
The Good News
Lord knows that this year
Has been empty
Of good news
The Trump shutdown
Passing its seventh day
An event with
No end in sight
Could go on
For another week
Another month
For all we know
The crazy man
In the White House
Wants his wall
The zealot in me
Says no wall
Ever
The craziness should end
Here and now
The realist in me
Says compromise
In the long run
Most people will say
Fuck it
Its only 4 billion
Let him have it

What's the big deal
The Dems are being stubborn
They will focus on drugs
And terrorism
And not on the people
The real human living people
Seeking refuge from
Gangs and violence
In Honduras El Salvador
Guatemala
And the people
That big splash of red
All across these states
The other half that lives
In their FOX holes
Afraid of Others
Will fix their blame
On those of us who say
No more bullshit
So maybe this is where
We will end this book
This long-ass poem
This sad-faced poem
This book of disasters
In a day or two
End it here
With a shutdown
A standoff
Standoffish
Don't make me commit
Don't commit me
This is the end
(but not the end)
Let Jim Morrison
Sing us to sleep
My friend
My beautiful friend
I want to wrap
This up for you
Wrap it up

On the fifth day of Christmas
Five golden rings
With a nice big bow
A perfect happy wisdom
But

12.30
On the way home
I decide to make
Another stop
In Greensboro
It's a little
Out of the way
Colleen wants
To get home
To spend time
With Jacob tonight
Since he will be
Driving to Atlanta
Tomorrow for a party
And then on
To Birmingham
To work
To make some money
For the spring semester
It is kind of boring
For him at home
Not really his home
Not where he grew up
Just where his parents
Moved after
He went to college
This is the town
We drove through
In August
And I didn't
Have time to find
Randall Jarrell's grave
Thought I would

End this year
With one more try
I tell Colleen
I will hurry
As in August
Cemetery easy to find
Sharing parking lot
With church
Sunday early afternoon
A few people
Still around
I head toward
The graves
Wandering for me
Is the best method
Like walking into
The stacks
Of a library
And trusting
I will find the book
I have been wanting
Colleen purposely
Calls over to a youngish
Middle-aged woman
Touches of gray
Stride to her walk
Say like the woman
At the Washington Zoo
Say like the woman
In the grocery store
Among the Cheer and Joy
The Joy and the All
Thinking about
Her friend's funeral
But I walk through
The gap in the hedges
Into the stark spaces
Because I know
His stone is flat
And thirty feet

In front of me
Is a mockingbird
   All day
   The mockingbird
   Has owned
   The yard
Tiptoeing in the grass
Beaking into blades
Alerting its head
Eyeing December
Quiet in his midday
Lunch
And no kidding
When I step
Toward it
There near the bird's
Shadow's eruption
From the ground
Are Randall's
And Mary's
And her mother's graves
Large slabs flat
Like granite cellar doors
On his
   Poet
   Teacher
   Beloved Husband
Pretty good description
I think
Good enough for me
If others so believed
Maybe add
   Proud Father
   Or
   Honored Father
That would be nice
And then the staring
At it for a while
Noticing the dew
Still staining the words

Only the area
Around the words
Like they were sweating
But it's December
Like they were bleeding
Then the shuffling
Of feet begins
Because what does
One do after
One finds the grave
It's the searching
The determination
The luck and mystery
That provide
The meaning
I think about war
The greatest generation
About casualties losses
And hosings
About girls in libraries
Bats and owls
And mockingbirds
Young boys in Hollywood
And a friezed Ganymede
Serving wine
In Nashville
I think about
Roadside choices
Or accidents
And lines and voices
Replaying
   You know
   what I was,
   You see
   what I am
But tilting my head
Like a mocking bird
I see words
That I might
Remember longer

Than Randall's
Mary's epitaph's
First line
   Joyful Christian
Almost an oxymoron
A duet/dual voices
Worthy of any
Mocking bird

I leave the grave
Behind
And approach Colleen
She says
I'll come help now
I say
I have already found it
She says
Great, oh, this is Ellen
Guess what
She went to JMU
And lived in Harrisonburg
I say
Cool good to meet you
But did not tell her
About Mary and Randall
Or
   the mockingbird
   imitating life

12.31
Rainy and cold
Why should today
Be any different
Went to my first zazen
At Black's Run
Meditation Center
In the center
Of Harrisonburg
I could look at it
This way
It was a day
Of little mistakes
I choose to laugh
About this
Why shouldn't I make
   mistakes
And struggle a little
As the universe turns
I was the only person
There besides
The person who "runs"
The place
What should I call her
I don't know
She was generous
And slow with her time
Introducing me
To their expected behaviors
And my behavioral
   expectations
I think I am supposed
To hold on to the former
And let go of the latter
Do you care why
I went there
I will tell you anyway
This is my last day
Indulge me
One last time
Simple I want to bring
Meditation into my life
Formally
I have meditated before
Haven't you
Sit on the floor
Pretzel my legs
Once I could do that
Can't anymore
Form little circles

With my thumb
And forefinger
Close my eyes
Breathe
Read a few books
By Thich Nhat Hanh
Maybe do a walking
Meditation
In the woods
On Rose Mountain
Read Peter Matthiessen
I've done that
Have you
Well that's not
Exactly the way
They do it
At Blacks Run
Now I am ready
To go deeper
Whatever that means
Why do I want
To go deeper
Whatever that means
Because there's more
To this stinking life
Than I am experiencing
Isn't there
I hope you know
I am not ungrateful
I have had good work
As work goes
But it has been work
In institutions
Yes it has been sacred work
When it has been
At its best
Helping students write well
Which really means
Helping them organize
Their thoughts well

And respect their tools
That's a sacred thing
To do
Not merely a practical
Economic thing to do
Introducing students
To literature art music
Is a sacred thing
To do
Listening to them
And offering advice or not
Is a sacred thing to do
Writing poems and
Writing whatever
We call this book
I have been lucky
Privileged
To spend my life so
Occupied
I am grateful
I bow to the seven directions
But there is a place in me
That has not been touched
I am a turtle man
A cicada man
A knight in dented armor
Although I have been aware
I have been institutionalized
Encased in formal practices
Meant to define me
By convention
This book has been
One way to escape
Let's see
If I have the courage
To continue
Next year
I am going to read the gospels
I am going to study
The parables

I am going to meditate
I am going to fast
I am going to exercise
The body
I am going to write some
Poems without I
Besides loving my family
Those will be my goals
Those are my new
Year's revolutions
[no sic Sherlock]
Wish me well
It has been a hard year
Tomorrow it starts over again
So I will say goodbye
Like last year
I will not make it
To midnight
If you stayed awake
I hope you had
A joyous kiss
With somebody
You love
Be well
Thanks for reading this
I hope this year
You find something to do
That takes care of yourself
By the way
Trump has wished you
A happy new year
He is at the White House
Working hard tweeting
Breathe

Epilogue
"Lines from January 2019"

```
108 bell chimes
                    symbolize purification
                                    from 108 delusions and
            sufferings accumulated          in past year
                    a writer must be faithful
he doesn't yet know why
                                        America's favorite
                                commie
know-it-all
                        clueless
                                                GOP
                    tell me
with your one wild
                    and precious life
                                why can't we get a deal
                                what is it you plan to do
we're getting crushed
            paradise gone
                        except
                            for the fragment left
                                    in the soul
        giving water
                    to someone dying of thirst
                                            is illegal
for they shall
inherit the earth
                                        to live paycheck
                                        to paycheck
I am not sure
            the President
                                        fully understands
        This was              in no way   a concession

                    You look like you'd love

                        a free drink
```

Notes

Prologue: "Lines from December 2017"

Sen. Mitch McConnell. As quoted in CNN. 2 December 2017. Retrieved at http://transcripts.cnn.com/TRANSCRIPTS/1712/02/cnr.22.html

Billy Bush. As quoted in "Billy Bush to Trump: 'Yes, You Said That.'" By Brian Selter. CNN. 4 December 2017. Retrieved at https://money.cnn.com/2017/12/03/media/billy-bush-trump-tape-women/index.html

A.R. Ammons. from Tape from the Turn of the Year. As quoted in "The Great American Poet of Daily Chores." By Dan Chiasson. *The New Yorker*. 4 December 2018. Retrieved at https://www.newyorker.com/magazine/2017/12/04/the-great-american-poet-of-daily-chores

Eli Mosley. (An Army veteran who would latter identify himself to reporters as the "command soldier major of the 'alt-right'") As quoted by Vice, in "Inside UV's Response to a White-Power Rally." By Jack Stripling. *The Chronicle of Higher Education*. 1 December 2017.

Wendell Berry. As quoted "Choosing to Lose: Wendell Berry's Sustainable Activism." By Jeffrey Bilbro. *Upright Magazine*. 8 February 2017. Retrieved at http://www.upwritemagazine.com/home/2017/2/6/choosing-to-lose

Wendy Frank. As told to the Associated Press. "California Struggles to Gain on Fires as New Ones Appear Daily." National Public Radio.. By Scott Neuman, 8 December 2017. Retrieved from https://www.npr.org/sections/thetwo-way/2017/12/08/569344505/california-struggles-to-gain-on-fires-as-new-ones-appear-daily

Donald Trump. "Trump's 41 Most Eye-popping Lines from His Pensacola Speech" The Point. CNN. By Chris Silizza. 8 December 2017. Retrieved at https://www.cnn.com/2017/12/09/politics/trump-pensacola-speech-analysis/index.html

George Ciccariello-Maher. "After Texas Massacre, Drexel Prof. Asks: "What Makes White Men So Prone to This Kind of Behavior?'" Interview with Amy Goodman. *Democracy Now*. 5 November 2017. Retrieved at https://www.democracynow.org/2017/11/6/after_texas_massacre_drexel_prof_asks

Joseph Mohr and Franz Xaver Gruber. "Stille Nacht, heilege Nacht." 1833. Translated by John Freeman Young. 1859.

"In Major Blow to Free Internet, FCC Votes to Repeal Landmark Net Neutrality Rules." *Democracy Now.* 15 December 2017. Retrieved at https://www.democracynow.org/2017/12/15/headlines/in_major_blow_to_free_internet_fcc_votes_to_repeal_landmark_net_neutrality_rules

2018

1.1
Daft Punk with Paul Williams, "Touch." On *Random Access Memory* by Daft Punk. Columbia Records. 2013.
Paul Williams and Roger Nicols. "Rainy Days and Mondays." On *Carpenters* by Carpenters. A&M Records. 1971.
Robert Burns. Traditional version. "Auld Lang Syne."

1.2
Donald Trump. Twitter. @realdonaldtrump. 2 January 2018.
Danny Kirwan. "Bare Trees." On *Bare Trees* by Fleetwood Mac. Reprise Records. 1972.

1.6
Donald Trump. Twitter. @realdonaldtrump. 6 January 2018.

1.11
Donald Trump. As quoted in "Trump decries 'people from s***hole countries' coming to US, report says." Fox2News St. Louis. Retrieved at https://fox2now.com/2018/01/11/trump-decries-people-from-shole-countries-coming-to-us-report-says/

1.25
Michael S. Schmidt and Maggie Haberman. "Trump ordered Mueller's firing but was refused." *New York Times.* 25 January 2018. Retrieved at The Berkshire Eagle. https://www.berkshireeagle.com/stories/trump-ordered-muellers-firing-but-was-refused,530419

1.27
Aubrey Graham, Dwayne Carter, Cedric Carter, Anthony Palman, Kenza Samir, Noah Shebib, Tyler Williams. "HYFR (Hell Ya Fucking Right." *Aspire.* 2012.

2.4
Luke 2:32. Bible. New International Version.

2.27
Donald Trump. As reported by David Jackson. "Trumps Rips Officers over Florida Shooting: 'I Really Believed I'd Run in there Even If I Didn't Have a Weapon." *USA Today*. 26 February 2018. Retrieved at https://www.usatoday.com/story/news/politics/2018/02/26/trump-says-he-would-have-confronted-florida-school-shooter-even-without-gun/372792002/

3.7
Chris Cilliza. "Donald Trump's alias and 7 other 'wow' moments from the Stormy Daniels lawsuit." *CNN*. 7 March 2018. Retrieved at https://www.cnn.com/2018/03/07/politics/trump-stormy-daniels-lawsuit/index.html
Tony Cook. "Pence used personal email for state business — and was hacked." *Indy Star*. 2 March 2017. Retrieved at https://www.indystar.com/story/news/politics/2017/03/02/pence-used-personal-email-state-business----and-hacked/98604904/

3.9
A.R. Ammons. *Tape for the Turn of the Year*. New York: W.W Norton. 1965.

3.14
Natasha Bach. "What You Need to Know About Wednesday's Massive Student Walk-Out." *Fortune*. 14 March 2018. Retrieved at http://fortune.com/2018/03/13/school-walkout-march-14-gun-control/
Don West. *No Lonesome Road: Selected Prose and Poems*. University of Illinois Press. 2004.

3.17
Donald Trump. Twitter. @realDonaldTrump. 17 March 2018.

3.24
Cassandra Batie and Adrian Gurvitz. "Rise Up." *On Cheers to the Fall*. Andra Day. Warner Brothers. 2015.
Cassandra Batie and Adrian Gurvitz. "Rise Up." On Cheers to the

Fall. Andra Day. Warner Brothers. 2015.

David Hogg. March for Our Lives. Washington D.C. 24 March 2018.

Victor Mensa, Larrance Dopson, Malik Jones, Glenda Proby, and Tyron Griffin, Jr. "We Could Be Free." *On The Autobiography*. Vic Mensa. Roc Nation. 2017.

Alex Wind. March for Our Lives. Washington D.C. 24 March 2018.

Lin-Manuel Miranda and Ben Platt. "Found/Tonight." At *Hamildrops*. Retrieved at http://www.hamildrops.com

Alex Wind. March for Our Lives. Washington D.C. 24 March 2018.

Cameron Kasky. March for Our Lives. Washington D.C. 24 March 2018.

Toby Gad, Lindy Robbins, and Kerli Koiv. "Skyscraper." On *Unbroken*. Demi Lavato. Hollywood. 2011.

Naomi Wadler. March for Our Lives. Washington D.C. 24 March 2018.

Cameron Kasky. March for Our Lives. Washington D.C. 24 March 2018.

Lin-Manuel Miranda and Ben Platt. "Found/Tonight." At *Hamildrops*. Retrieved at http://www.hamildrops.com

Toby Gad, Lindy Robbins, and Kerli Koiv. "Skyscraper." On *Unbroken*. Demi Lavato. Hollywood. 2011.

Emma Gonzalez. March for Our Lives. Washington D.C. 24 March 2018.

4.2

Cynthia Littleton. "Sinclair Responds to Promo Critics, Says Fake News Warnings 'Serve No Political Agenda.'" *Variety*. 2 April 2018.

4.10

MarketWatch. "Full Transcript of Trump's Comments Following FBI Raid on Cohen's Office. 9 April 2018. Retrieved at https://www.marketwatch.com/story/full-transcript-of-trumps-comments-following-fbi-raid-on-cohens-office-2018-04-09

4.14

Donald Trump. Twitter. @realDonaldTrump. 14 April 2018

4/26

Fox News. "President Trumps Talks North Korea, Iran, Comey, Cohen, Dr. Ronny Jackson and Kanye West in 'Fox & Friends Interview." 26 April 2018. Retrieved at https://www.foxnews.com/transcript/president-trump-talks-north-korea-iran-comey-cohen-dr-ronny-jackson-and-kanye-west-in-fox-friends-interview

5.9

Gregory Krieg. "What Gina Haspel Didn't Tell Us at Her High-Stakes CIA Hearing." CNN. 9 May 2018. Retrieved at https://www.cnn.com/2018/05/09/politics/gina-haspel-cia-hearing-unanswered-questions/index.html

5/11

James Madison. Wednesday 6 June 1787. Madison Debates. The Avalon Project. Yale Law School. Lillian Goldman Law Library. Retrieved at http://avalon.law.yale.edu/18th_century/debates_606.asp

James Madison Montpelier. "The Mere Distinction of Colour." Retrieved at https://www.montpelier.org/learn/6-ways-that-understanding-slavery-will-change-how-you-understand-american-freedom

5/13

George Will. "Pence Is a Model of Governing by Groveling." *St. Louis Post-Dispatch*. 11 May 2018. Retrieved at https://www.stltoday.com/opinion/columnists/national/george-will-pence-is-a-model-of-governing-by-groveling/article_ad500866-d774-5cbd-a6f5-481e0b93479b.html

Laura Hollis. "The Tyranny of Elites. 10 May 2018. Creator.com. Retrieved at https://www.creators.com/read/laura-hollis/05/18/the-tyranny-of-the-elites

5.14

Gina C. Haspel. Letter to Senator Mark Warner. 14 May 2018. CNN. Retrieved at https://www.cnn.com/2018/05/15/politics/read-haspel-letter-warner/index.html

6.3

Vox. "Sexual Harassment Assault Allegations List." 3 June 2018. Retrieved at https://www.vox.com/a/sexual-harassment-assault-allegations-list/

6/15

Lisa Page. As quoted in Tucker Higgins. "FBI Agent's text disclosed by Justice watchdog: 'We'll stop Trump from becoming president." CNBC. 14 June 2018. Retrieved at https://www.cnbc.com/2018/06/14/fbi-agents-text-reportedly-disclosed-by-justice-watchdog-well-stop-trump-from-becoming-president.html

Peter Strzok. As quoted in Tucker Higgins. "FBI Agent's text disclosed by Justice watchdog: 'We'll stop Trump from becoming president." CNBC. 14 June 2018. Retrieved at https://www.cnbc.com/2018/06/14/fbi-agents-text-reportedly-disclosed-by-justice-watchdog-well-stop-trump-from-becoming-president.html

Amy Berman Jackson. As quoted in Katelyn Polantz. "Judge sends Paul Manafort to jail, pending trial." CNN. 16 June 2018. Retrieved at https://www.cnn.com/2018/06/15/politics/judge-sends-paul-manafort-to-jail-pending-trial/index.html

Donald Trump. Twitter. @realDonaldTrump. 13 June 2018.

Donald Trump. As quoted in Katelyn Polantz. "Judge sends Paul Manafort to jail, pending trial." CNN. 16 June 2018. Retrieved at https://www.cnn.com/2018/06/15/politics/judge-sends-paul-manafort-to-jail-pending-trial/index.html

Rudolf Giuliani. As quoted in Autumn Brewington, et al. "Nine Takeaways from the Inspector General's Report on the Clinton Email Investigation." *Law Fare*. 14 June 2018. Retrieved at https://www.lawfareblog.com/nine-takeaways-inspector-generals-report-clinton-email-investigation

Ronna McDaniel. As quoted in S. E. Cupp. "Cupp: RNC chair's tweet spells doom for the party I love." CNN. 14 June 2018. Retrieved at https://www.cnn.com/2018/06/14/opinions/ronna-mcdaniel-tweet-is-the-death-of-the-gop-cupp-opinion/index.html

Rachel Maddow. *The Rachel Maddow Show*. 15 June 2018. Retrieved at https://archive.org/details MSN-BCW_20180616_040000_The_Rachel_Maddow_Show

6.21
John Moore. Photographer. CBSNews. Retrieved at https://www.cbsnews.com/pictures/recommended/

6.22-6.30
Donald Trump. Twitter. @realDonaldTrump. 26 June 2018.
Donald Trump. Twitter. @realDonaldTrump. 27 June 2018.
Donald Trump. Twitter. @realDonaldTrump. 30 June 2018

7.4
Jefferson, Thomas, et al. The Declaration of Independence.
John. Kline. "The Prisoner's Song." In Sanger, Samuel F. and Daniel Hays. *The Olive Branch of Peace and Good Will to Men.* Elgin, IL: Brethren Publishing House. 1907. pp. 156-58.

7.10.
Neville Morgan, Dir. With Fred Rogers. *Will You Be My Neighbor?* Focus Features Film. 2018.

7.12-7.13
Italo Calvino. "The Naked Bosom." *Mr. Palomar.* Tr. William Weaver. San Diego: Harcourt Brace. 1983.
Cliff, Chambers, Jimmy Holiday and James Lewis. "The Girls from Texas." *Borderline.* Warner Bros. 1980.

7.14
Hannah Arendt. *The Life of the Mind.* New York: Harcourt Brace Jovanovich. 1978.
Hannah Arendt. *Origins of Totalitarianism.* New York: Schocken Books. 1951
Hannah Arendt. *Eichmann in Jerusalem.* New York: Viking. 1963.
George Randall Leake, III. Facebook Post. 14 July 2018.

7.15-7.20
Terence (Publius Terentius Afer). Fom *Heauton Timorumenos.* "*Homo sum, humani nihil a me alienum puto,*" translated asI am human, and I think nothing human is alien to me."[1]
Hannah Arendt. "Willing." *From The Life of the Mind.* New York: Harcourt Brace Jovanovich. 1978.

7.22

Donald Trump. As reported in Foreign Policy. 18 July 2018. Retrieved at https://foreignpolicy.com/2018/07/18/heres-what-trump-and-putin-actually-said-in-helsinki/

Donald Trump. As reported by Kate Lyons. "Would or wouldn't: how Trump's claim he misspoke unleashed a meme-fest." *The Guardian*. 18 July 2018. Retrieved at https://www.theguardian.com/us-news/2018/jul/19/would-or-wouldnt-how- trumps-claim-he-misspoke-unleashed-a-meme-fest

7.28.

E. D. Hirsch. *Cultural Literacy: What Every American Needs to Know.* New York: Random House. 1988.

Thomas Hobbes. *Leviathan.* New York: Penguin Classics. 1985.

John Locke. *Second Treatise of Government.* Indianapolis: Hackett. 1980.

Jean Jacques Rousseau. *The Social Contract.* New York: Penguin Classics. 1968.

Mary Wollstonecraft. *A Vindication of the Rights of Women.* New York: Norton Critical Editions. 2009.

Voltaire. *Candide.* New York: Norton Critical Editions. 2016.

John Milton. *Paradise Lost.* New York: Penguin Classics. 2000

Alexander Pope. "Epistle II." Essay on Man. Retrieved from Poetry Foundation. https://www.poetryfoundation.org/poems/44900/an-essay-on-man-epistle-ii

Moliere. *Le Bourgeois Gentilhomme.* Charles Heron Wall, Tr. Wolf Pup Books. 2010.

7.30

Truman Capote. Interview. *The Paris Review.* Spring-Summer 1957.

8.12-8.17

John Brennan. "What responsible…" Twitter. @JohnBrennan. 4 August 2018.

Donald Trump. "While I know…" Twitter. @realDonaldTrump. 13 August 2018

John Brennan. "You're absolutely right…" Twitter. @JohnBrennan. 13 August 2018

Donald Trump. "When you give…" Twitter. @realDonaldTrump.

14 August 2018

John Brennan. "It's astounding…" Twitter. @JohnBrennan. 14 August 2018.

Donald Trump. "As your president…" As reported at Fox News. "Trump's full statement on revoking John Brennan's security clearance." 15 August 2018.

John Brennan. "This action…"Twitter. @JohnBrennan. 15 August 2018.

William McCraven. "You have revoked…" In Felicia Sonmez. *The Washington Post*. 17 August 2018. Reprinted at "McRaven: 'I would consider it an honor if you would revoke my security clearance as well.'" The Stars and Stripes. Retrieved at: https://www.stripes.com/news/us/mcraven-i-would-consider-it-an-honor-if-you-would-   revoke-my-security-clearance-as-well-1.543055

175 former US officials. "All of us believe…". CNN. "175 former US officials added to list denouncing Trump for revoking Brennan's security clearance." NBC26 Green Bay. 20 August 2018. Retrieved at https://www.nbc26.com/news/national-politics/175-former-us-officials-added-to-list-denouncing-trump-for-revoking-brennans-security-clearance

8.22
Donald Trump. Twitter. @realDonaldTrump. 22 August 2018.

9.8
Ann Banks. "Dirty Trick, South Carolina, and John McCain." *The Nation*. 14 January 2008. Retrieved at https://www.thenation.com/article/dirty-tricks-south-carolina-and-john-mccain/

Megan McCain. Eulogy. Retrieved at https://www.townandcountrymag.com/society/politics/a22892378/meghan-mccain-eulogy-for-john-mccain-full-transcript/

Joseph Lieberman. Eulogy. Retrieved at https://www.townandcountrymag.com/society/politics/a22892540/joe-lieberman-john-mccain-memorial-speech-full-transcript/

Henry Kissinger. Eulogy. Retrieved at https://www.townandcountrymag.com/society/politics/a22892548/henry-kissinger-eulogy-for-john-mccain-full-transcript/

George W. Bush. Eulogy. Retrieved at https://www.townandcountrymag.com/society/politics/a22865864/george-w-bush-john-mccain-funeral-speech-eulogy-full-transcript/

Barack Obama. Eulogy. Retrieved at https://www.theatlantic.com/politics/archive/2018/09/barack-obama-eulogy-john-mccain/569065/

Ernest Hemingway. *For Whom the Bell Tolls.* New York: Scribners. 1940.

9.9

Donald Trump. Twitter. @realDonaldTrump. 9 September 2018.

9.13

Donald Trump. Twitter. @realDonaldTrump. 13 September 2018.

9.20

Donald Trump. "One of the wettest we've seen from the standpoint of water." Video. *The Guardian.* 19 September 2018. Retrieved at https://www.theguardian.com/us-news/video/2018/sep/19/one-of-the-wettest-weve-ever-seen-from-the-standpoint-of-water-trump-on-florence-video

Donald Trump. "Donald Trump on brett kavanaugh's accuser: 'I really want to hear what she has to say.'" Video. *The Guardian.* 19 September 2018. Retrieved at https://www.theguardian.com/us-news/video/2018/sep/19/donald-trump-on-brett-kavanaughs-accuser-i-really-want-to-hear-what-she-has-to-say-video

10.9

Email to author from HR Department, Eastern Mennonite University.

10.11

Donald Trump. "Remarks by President Trump in Meeting with Kanye West and Jim Brown. The White House. 1 October 2018. Retrieved at https://www.whitehouse.gov/briefings-statements/remarks-president-trump-meeting-kanye-west-jim-brown/

Kanye West. Reported by Raisa Bruner. "Here's What Kanye West Said to President Trump at the White House." *Time.* 11 October 2018. Retrieved at http://time.com/5422270/kanye-west-trump-speech/

Jim Brown. "Remarks by President Trump in Meeting with Kanye

West and Jim Brown. The White House. 1 October 2018. Retrieved at https://www.whitehouse.gov/briefings-statements/remarks-president-trump-meeting-kanye-west-jim-brown/

10.17

Donald Trump. Twitter. @ealDonaldTrump. 16 October 2018.

Bethan McKernan and Julian Borger. "Khashoggi: Trump defends Saudi Arabia as Pompeo heads to Turkey." *The Guardian*. 17 October 2018. Retrieved at https://www.theguardian.com/world/2018/oct/16/jamal-khashoggi-disappearance-mike-pompeo-saudi-arabia-salman

10.19

Email to author from HR Department at Eastern Mennonite University.

10.23

Donald Trump. As quoted by Chris Cillizza. "Donald Trump used a word he's 'not supposed to.' Here's why." CNN. 23 October 2018. Retrieved at https://www.cnn.com/2018/10/23/politics/donald-trump-nationalism/index.html

10.31

Kanye West. Reported by Itay Hod. "Kanye West Renounces Politics: 'I've Been Used to Spread Messages I Don't Believe In." *The Wrap*. 30 October 2018. Retrieved at https://www.thewrap.com/kanye-west-renounces-politics-ive-used-spread-messages-dont-believe/

11.15

Donald Trump. Twitter. @realDonaldTrump. 15 November 2018.

11.17

Jon Meacham. *The Soul of America: The Battle for Our Better Angels*. New York: Random House, 2018

11.18

Gabriel Faure. Requiem. Text based on the Catholic Mass for the Dead. Retrieved at http://lyricbod.blogspot.com/2009/02/requiem-gabriel-faure.html

12.6

Jon Meacham. Eulogy. Retrieved at https://www.townandcountrymag.com/society/politics/a25412042/jon-meacham-george-hw-bush-funeral-eulogy-transcript/

Donald Trump. Speech. Reported by Ian Schwartz. "Trump: What The Hell Is 'Thousand Points Of Light?'; We Understand 'Make America Great Again.'" 6 July 2018. Real Clear Politics. Retrieved at https://www.realclearpolitics.com/video/2018/07/06/trump_what_the_hell_is_thousand_points_of_light_we_understand_make_america_great_again.html

Alan Simpson. Eulogy. Retrieved at https://www.townandcountrymag.com/society/politics/a25412509/alan-simpson-george-hw-bush-funeral-eulogy-transcript/

Donald Trump. Interview. *Face the Nation.* Retrieved at https://www.cbsnews.com/video/donald-trump-i-have-more-humility-than-you-would-think/

George W. Bush. Eulogy. Retrieved at https://www.upi.com/Top_News/Voices/2018/12/06/Full-text-Former-President-George-W-Bushs-eulogy-for-his-father/3661544105842/ Donald Trump.

Donald Trump. Access Hollywood Tape. Reported by Rachael Revesz. "Full transcript: Donald Trump's lewd remarks about women on Days of Our Lives set in 2005." Independent. 7 October 2016. Retrieved at https://www.independent.co.uk/news/world/americas/read-donald-trumps-lewd-remarks-about-women-on-days-of-our-lives-set-2005-groping-star-a7351381.html

12.7

Rex Tillerson. Interview. Retrieved at. https://www.cbs.com/shows/cbs_this_morning/video/H5oesSXvET08JdpxLi-IASZssk_rZlwU4/rex-tillerson-opens-up-on-trump-and-his-firing-we-did-not-have-a-common-value-system-/

Donald Trump. Twitter. @realDonaldTrump. 7 December 2018.

12.20

Lines from Brandon Griggs. *Living while Black.* CNN. Retrieved at https://www.cnn.com/2018/12/20/us/living-while-black-police-calls-trnd/index.html

12.21
Henry Wadsworth Longfellow. "The Building of the Ship."

12.24
Donald Trump. Twitter. @realDonaldTrump. 24 December 2018.

12.26
Wendell Berry. "Our Christmas tree is" Sabbath Poem, *1996, no. VIII. A Timbered Choir: The Sabbath Poems, 1979-1997.* New York: Counterpoint Press. 1998.

12.30
Randall Jarrell. "The Woman at the Washington Zoo." *The Complete Poems.* New York: Farrar, Straus & Giroux. 1969.
Randall Jarrell. "Next Day." *The Complete Poems.* New York: Farrar, Straus & Giroux. 1969.
Randall Jarrell. "The Mockingbird." *The Complete Poems.* New York: Farrar, Straus & Giroux. 1969.

Epilogue: "Lines from January 2019"
"New Year in Japan—108 Bell Chimes." Maza-chan's Gateway to Japan. 31 December 2009. Retrieved at https://muza-chan.net/japan/index.php/blog/new-year-in-japan-108
A R Ammons. Interview by Philip Fried. Terrain. Rog. 22 October 2009. Retrieved at https://www.terrain.org/2009/interviews/a-r-ammons/?fbclid=IwAR2aQovhmcPg-9mUVyFyeOYEo-sG9-fxf7MxtxcSnuJQTfG1QTGLC-yx_qA
Faith Karimi. "Alexandra Ocasio-Cortez responds to dance video critics with more dancing." CNN. 4 January 2019. Retrieved at https://www.cnn.com/2019/01/04/politics/ocasio-cortez-dancing-video-trnd/index.html
Mary Oliver. "The Summer Day." Quoted in Lynn Neary. "Beloved Poet Mary Oliver Who Believed Poetry 'Mustn't Be Fancy,' Dies at 83." NPR. 17 January 2019. Retrieved at. https://www.npr.org/2019/01/17/577380646/beloved-poet-mary-oliver-who-believed-poetry-mustn-t-be-fancy-dies-at-83
Donald Trump. Quoting Donald Trump. "Trump Vents to Mulvaney: 'We're Getting Crushed' on Shutdown Coverage." TPM. 17 January 2019. Retrieved at https://

talkingpointsmemo.com/news/trump-shutdown-we-are-getting-crushed

Jonas Mekas, Dir. A Walk. 1990. Retrieved at https://www.youtube.com/watch?v=_qj-LMIsM8c

Catherine Gaffney. Quoted in Ray Sanchez. "Volunteers face prison after leaving food and water in desert where migrants died." CNN. 22 January 2019. Retrieved at https://www.cnn.com/2019/01/22/us/arizona-aid-volunteers-guilty-trespassing-trnd/index.html

"The Sermon on the Mount." Matthew 5:5. King James Version.

Susan Collins. Reported by John Bowden. "GOP Sen. Collins: I'm not sure the president understands living 'paycheck to paycheck. *The Hill*. 25 January 2019. Retrieved at https://thehill.com/homenews/senate/426924-gop-senator-im-not-sure-that-the-president-fully-understands-what-its-like-to

Donald Trump. Twitter. @realDonaldTrump. 25 January 2019.

Starbucks In-store Sign. Starbucks. Interstate 81. 19 January 2019.

Acknowledgements

Portions of this book were published, some in slightly different forms, in *Five Friends—Sunday Afternoons*: "2.4" as "Snow"; "4.1" as "Pancakes"; "5.3" as "Doubt"; "6.12" as "Brakes"; "7.30" as "Storm"; and "8.30" as "Sky."

Lyman would like to thank Lowell Mick White and Pamela Booton at Alamo Bay Press for their support and care with this book. In dark days, they keep the lights on.

About Lyman Grant

Lyman Grant is a poet living in Harrisonburg, Virginia. *2018: Found Poems and Weather Reports* is his seventh collection of poems. Previous work includes *Old Men on Tuesday Mornings* (also by Alamo Bay Press), *As Long as We Need* (Black Buzzard Press), and *The Road Home* (Dalton Press). His essays, reviews, and poems have been published in many journals and anthologies, including *Dallas Morning News, Texas Humanist, Texas Observer, descant, RE:AL, Concho River Review, Sulphur River Literary Review, Langdon Review,* and *Big Land Big Sky Big Hair.* He attended both the Bread Loaf Writers' Conference and the Sewanee Writers' Conference. In addition, his work been nominated several times for the Pushcart Prize and won first place in *The Great American Wise Ass Anthology*. He has degrees from The University of Texas and Texas A&M University, and has worked at Austin Community College for over 40 years as professor, department chair, and as dean.